JAVASCRIPT FROM ZERO TO PROFICIENT
(BEGINNER)

A step-by-step guide to learn JavaScript.

Patrick Felicia

JavaScript From Zero To Proficiency (Beginner)

Copyright © 2018 Patrick Felicia

All rights reserved. No part of this book may be reproduced, stored in retrieval systems, or transmitted in any form or by any means, without the prior written permission of the publisher (Patrick Felicia), except in the case of brief quotations embedded in critical articles or reviews.

Every effort has been made in the preparation of this book to ensure the accuracy of the information presented. However, the information contained in this book is sold without warranty, either expressed or implied. Neither the author and its dealers and distributors will be held liable for any damages caused or alleged to be caused directly or indirectly by this book.

First published: July 2018

Published by Patrick Felicia

CREDITS

Author: Patrick Felicia.

Technical Reviewer: Jose Luis Soler Dominguez

Patrick Felicia is a lecturer and researcher at Waterford Institute of Technology, where he teaches and supervises undergraduate and postgraduate students. He obtained his MSc in Multimedia Technology in 2003 and PhD in Computer Science in 2009 from University College Cork, Ireland. He has published several books and articles on the use of video games for educational purposes, including the Handbook of Research on Improving Learning and Motivation through Educational Games: Multidisciplinary Approaches (published by IGI), and Digital Games in Schools: a Handbook for Teachers, published by European Schoolnet. Patrick is also the Editor-in-chief of the International Journal of Game-Based Learning (IJGBL), and the Conference Director of the Irish Symposium on Game-Based Learning, a popular conference on games and learning organized throughout Ireland. He has also published books on coding with C# through the creation of games.

Jose Luis Soler Dominguez is a senior lecturer and PhD researcher at Florida University (Spain). he has a wide experience in the software development area (first as a coder and after as project manager) and Business Intelligence Consultancy. He is currently lecturing about Game Design, Game Technology and Serious Games.

Books from the same author

Unity 5 from Zero to Proficiency (Foundations): In this book, you will become more comfortable with Unity's interface and its core features by creating a project that includes both an indoor and an outdoor environment. This book only covers drag and drop features, so that you are comfortable with Unity's interface before starting to code (in the next book). After completing this book, you will be able to create outdoors environments with terrains and include water, hills, valleys, sky-boxes, use built-in controllers (First- and Third-Person controllers) to walk around the 3D environment and also add and pilot a car and an aircraft.

Unity 5 from Zero to Proficiency (Beginner): In this book, you will get started with coding using JavaScript. The book provides an introduction to coding for those with no previous programming experience, and it explains how to use JavaScript in order to create an interactive environment. Throughout the book, you will be creating a game, and also implementing the core mechanics through scripting. After completing this book, you will be able to write code in JavaScript, understand and apply key programming principles, understand and avoid common coding mistakes, learn and apply best programming practices, and build solid programming skills.

Unity 5 from Zero to Proficiency (Intermediate): In this book, you improve your coding skills and learn more programming concepts to add more activity to your game while optimizing your code. The book provides an introduction to coding in C# t. Throughout the book, you will be creating a game, and also implementing the core mechanics through scripting. After completing this book, you will be able to write code in C#, understand and apply Object-Oriented Programming techniques in C#, create and use your own classes, use Unity's Finite State Machines, and apply intermediate Artificial Intelligence.

Unity 5 from Zero to Proficiency (Advanced): In this book, which is the last in the series, you will go from Intermediate to Advanced and get to work on more specific topics to improve your games and their performances. After completing this book, you will be able to create a (networked) multi-player game, access Databases from Unity, understand and apply key design, patterns for game development, use your time more efficiently to create games, structure and manage a Unity project efficiently, optimize game performances, optimize the structure of your game, and create levels procedurally.

Support and Resources for this Book

A companion website has been set-up for this book, it includes several code solutions and samples for each of the chapters in this book.

To avail of this content, you can open the following link:

http://learnjavascriptforbeginners.wordpress.com/

This site also provides you with the opportunity to subscribe to a newsletter, to obtain exclusive discounts and offers on new books, and to also receive a free copy of this book in the pdf format.

Why should you subscribe?

- Be the first to be notified of new resources available.
- Receive regular updates and tutorials on JavaScript.
- Receive a newsletter with tips and hints on JavaScript.

This book is dedicated to Helena & Mathis

Preface

This book is part of a series entitled **JavaScript from Zero to Proficiency**. In this book series, you have the opportunity to learn JavaScript programming from scratch and to become proficient in this popular scripting language.

In this book entitled "**JavaScript from Zero to Proficiency (Beginner)**" you will discover how to quickly get started with JavaScript; you will learn about how to use variables, functions, conditional statements and you will also write your first scripts.

WHAT YOU NEED TO USE THIS BOOK

To complete the project presented in this book, you only need a text editor such as Notepad, Notepad+ or Sublime and a web browser such as Mozilla Firefox.

In terms of computer skills, all the knowledge introduced in this book will assume no prior programming experience from the reader. Although this book includes scripting, you will be guided step-by-step. So for now, you only need to be able to perform common computer tasks such as typing, and opening and saving files.

WHO THIS BOOK IS FOR

If you can answer **yes** to all these questions, then this book is for you:

- Are you a total beginner in JavaScript programming?

- Would you like to get started fast with JavaScript concepts?

- Although you may have had some prior exposure to JavaScript, would you like to delve more into JavaScript and add interactivity to your pages through scripting?

If you can answer yes to all these questions, then this book is **not** for you:

- Can you already easily code in JavaScript?

- Are you looking for a reference book on JavaScript?

- Are you an experienced (or at least advanced) JavaScript programmer?

If you can answer yes to these three questions, you may instead look for other books in this series. To see the content and topics covered by these books, you can check the official website: **http://www.learnjavascriptforbeginners.wordpress.com**.

IMPROVING THE BOOK

Although great care was taken in checking the content of this book, I am human, and some errors could remain in the book. As a result, it would be great if you could let me know of any issue or error you may have come across in this book, so that it can be solved and the book updated accordingly. To report an error, you can email me (learnjavascriptforbeginners@gmail.com) with the following information:

- Name of the book.

- The page where the error was detected.

- Describe the error and also what you think the correction should be.

Once your email is received, the error will be checked, and, in the case of a valid error, it will be corrected and the book page will be updated to reflect the changes accordingly.

SUPPORTING THE AUTHOR

A lot of work has gone into this book and it is the fruit of long hours of preparation, brainstorming, and finally writing. As a result, I would ask that you do not distribute any illegal copies of this book.

This means that if a friend wants a copy of this book, s/he will have to buy it through the official channels (i.e., through Amazon, lulu.com, or the book's official website: **www.learnjavascriptforbeginners.wordpress.com/**.

If some of your friends are interested in the book, you can refer them to the book's official website (**http://www.learnjavascriptforbeginners.wordpress.com/**) where they can either buy the book, enter a monthly draw to be in for a chance of receiving a free copy of the book, or to be notified of future promotional offers.

TABLE OF CONTENTS

1 Introduction to Programming in JavaScript 1
    What is JavaScript 2
    HTML and JavaScript 3
    Choosing a code editor 5
    Browser Compatibility 6
    Creating your first page 7
    Introduction to JavaScript Syntax 10
    statements 11
    Comments 13
    Variables 15
    Operators 18
    Conditional statements 20
    Functions 25
    Scope of variables 28
    Using the Console window 30
    Storing all scripts in one file 33
    A few things to remember when you create a script (checklist) 34
    Common errors and Best Practices 35
    Level roundup 37

2 Objects & Structures 42
    Working with string variables 43
    Working with number variables 47
    Switch Statements 49
    Loops 52
    Arrays 55
    Working with dates 61
    Objects 65
    Constructors 67
    Modifying Objects 69
    Level roundup 71

3 Adding Interaction 76
    Processing events 77
    Accessing HTML elements from JavaScript 80
    Using JavaScript with forms (Part 1) 83
    Using JavaScript with forms (Part 2) 86
    Validating Forms with the forms API 89
    Event Listeners 92
    Bubbling and Capturing Events 94
    Navigating through nodes 97
    Adding and removing nodes and element 100
    Working with the browser 103
    Displaying information about the browser 104
    Opening, closing and moving windows from a script 106
    Working with the browser's location and history 109
    Level roundup 111

4 Thank you 116

1
INTRODUCTION TO PROGRAMMING IN JAVASCRIPT

In this section you will discover some programming principles and concepts, so that you can start programming in the next chapter. If you have already coded using JavaScript (or a similar language), you can skip this chapter.

After completing this chapter, you will be able to:

- Understand basic programming concepts.

- Become comfortable with variables and functions.

- Understand conditional statements and Boolean logic.

- Understand some of the best practices for coding.

WHAT IS JAVASCRIPT

JavaScript is a scripting language that makes it possible to add interaction to web pages. JavaScript is usually embedded in a web page and executed within the browser; this why it is called a client-side scripting language, as it is executed in the browser (the client) rather than on a server.

JavaScript is often referred as ECMAScript; this is because while JavaScript was invented by Brendan Eich as a scripting language, ECMAScript is a standard for scripting languages, and JavaScript implements some of the features and specifications defined by ECMAScript.

JavaScript has the ability to access and amend the content of a web page; for example, with JavaScript, you can check the content of text fields, and you can display alert boxes and messages in the console window.

This being said, JavaScript also makes it possible to communicate with a server through technologies often referred as AJAX, whereby information is sent asynchronously to the server, and then processed accordingly.

JavaScript is usually embedded in an HTML file so that it can be executed by the browser; so in order to code your first JavaScript programme, you may need to have some understanding of HTML.

HTML AND JAVASCRIPT

Before we start with JavaScript, let's look at the structure of an HTML file to get to understand how JavaScript and HTML work together.

When you open a page on the internet, it is probably an HTML page. HTML stands for Hyper Text Markup Language and is a language that is used to define the content of a page. It consists of nested nodes organized hierarchically. After reading the HTML code for a page, the browser will in turn display its content as specified in the HTML file.

An HTML document usually includes two key parts call the **head** and the **body**, and that can typically be structured as described in the next code snippet:

```
<!DOCTYPE html>
<HTML>
    <HEAD>
        <TITLE>My First HTML Page</TITLE>
    </HEAD>
    <BODY>
        Hello World<BR>
        Click here for Google.
    </BODY>
</HTML>
```

In the previous code:

- We declare the **doctype**, in our case, we will be using HTML5, and the corresponding doctype is HTML.

- We open the tag called **<HTML>** which corresponds to the entire document.

- We then include a nested tag called **<HEAD>** that will include information that will not be displayed on the page; for example, the title of the page, JavaScript code, or styling preferences.

- We then close the **HEAD** portion of the document using the tag **</HEAD>**

- We open the tag for the body **<BODY>** and add content that will be displayed on the page.

- We then close the body of the document using the tag **</BODY>**.

- We finally close the document using the tag **</HTML>**.

> HTML files are usually saved with the extension **.html**, or **.htm**.

From the code above, we can infer a few rules and good practices for HTML documents:

- Each opening tag has a corresponding closing tag (e.g. <HTML> and </HTML>)

- It is good practice to use tabulation to keep the code neat and easily readable. Corresponding opening and closing tags are usually tabulated at the same level.

- Each pair of corresponding tags is nested within the "parent" tag (e.g. BODY tags are both inside the HTML tags).

- The <HTML> section is the topmost container of an HTML document

- <HEAD>: This section will contain information about the style of the document, the scripts in this page and the title of the page. In general, it contains information that is not considered to be document content (i.e., information that is not meant to be displayed).

- <TITLE>: These tags identify the content of the document.

- <BODY>: These tags contain the content of the document (what will be visible).

-
: This tag includes a line break.

CHOOSING A CODE EDITOR

In the next sections, you will start to write your own JavaScript code. For this purpose, you will need to use a code editor.

Now, there are many code editors that you can use for this purpose, from very simple to sophisticated.

While simple text editors such as notepad are sufficient for JavaScript, more advanced code editors such as Sublime Text (my favorite), Atom, Brackets, or Vim might give you a significant advantage because they include, amongst other things, the following features that may speed-up the coding process:

- **Text highlighting**: so that you code is clearer to read and to modify.

- **Auto-completion**: so that you don't have to remember the name of all the variables in your code, or the name of some common functions.

- **Error highlighting**: so that some obvious errors are highlighted before you even test your code.

You can download some common and free editors using the following links:

- *Sublime Text*: https://www.sublimetext.com/

- *Atom*: https://atom.io/

- *Brackets*: http://brackets.io/

- *Vim*: https://www.vim.org/

BROWSER COMPATIBILITY

JavaScript can be used in most current browsers, although some don't implement all its features. The code presented in this book was written and tested in *FireFox 60* for Mac OS and it should work in your own browser. This being said, alternative code is provided in case of possible incompatibilities with some browsers.

CREATING YOUR FIRST PAGE

After this brief introduction to HTML, it is now your turn to code.

So that you get to experiment with your first HTML page, please do the following:

- Open a text editor of your choice. If you are using *Sublime Text*, select **File | New File** from the top menu.

- Type the following code in the new document:

```
<!DOCTYPE html>
<HTML>
    <HEAD>
        <TITLE>My First HTML Page</TITLE>

    </HEAD>

    <BODY>
        Hello World<BR>
        Next Line.
    </BODY>
</HTML>
```

In the previous code:

- We declare our document as **HTML5** thanks to the **doctype**.

- We then add a title to our document using the tag **<TITLE>** that is nested within the **<HEAD>** tag.

- After closing the **<HEAD>** tag, we then open the **<BODY>** tag and add some text that will be displayed onscreen.

- The text **Hello World** is followed by the tag **
** which corresponds to a line break.

- This line break is then followed by the text **Next Line**.

> Note that each nested tag has been indented using a tabulation so that corresponding opening and closing tags appear at the same level and to the right of its parent. This is a good practice for clear and easily understandable code. It is also a very good way to check that all your tags are properly closed.

Once you have typed these lines, we can then save the file:

- Save this file as **myFirstFile.html** in a location of your choice. If you are using *Sublime Text*, please select **File | Save As** from the top menu.

> When you save your HTML file, please ensure that use the extension *.html*, otherwise your computer will not know that this file is to be opened by a browser.

- Once the code has been saved, please open this file with your browser: navigate to the folder where you have saved the HTML file and double click on it, this should open the page in your default browser. Alternatively, you can left-click on the file and select the application that you'd like to use to open the file from the contextual menu.

- Once this is done, you should see a page in your browser with the title "My First HTML Page", along with some text in the body of the document, as illustrated in the next figure.

Figure 1-1: Opening your first HTML page

Now that we have a basic understanding of the structure of an HTML document, we can start to see how JavaScript can be added to this page.

Typically, JavaScript code is added to an HTML file using the **<SCRIPT>** tags. These tags can be added to the **HEAD** or **BODY** of the document.

- Please open the document **myFirstScript.html** that you have just created in the text editor of your choice.

- Add the new code (highlighted in bold) to this file.

```
<!DOCTYPE html>
<HTML>
    <HEAD>
        <TITLE>My First HTML Page</TITLE>
        <SCRIPT>
            alert("Hello from the head");
        </SCRIPT>

    </HEAD>

    <BODY>
        Hello World<BR>
        <SCRIPT>
            alert("Hello from the body");
        </SCRIPT>

    </BODY>
</HTML>
```

In the previous code:

- We add a script tag in the **HEAD** of our document. The code within these tags displays an alert box.

- The code is followed by a semicolon.

- We also add a <SCRIPT> tag in the **BODY** of our document. The code within these tags displays an alert box.

> Note that is some special circumstances, it may be preferable to use a script in the **BODY** of the document rather than the **HEAD** so that all HTML elements have been read and displayed by the browser before JavaScript code is executed.

- In both cases, the script will be executed by the browser.

> Also note that the previous code assume that you are enabling pop-up windows in your browser. In Internet explorer, this can be done using the menu **Tools | Options**, and in Mozilla Firefox, you just need to select the "hamburger" menu in the top-right corner, and then select **Options**.

Once you have updated the script, please save your changes (*CTRL + S*) and refresh the corresponding browser page (CTRL + R or APPLE+R) where your page is open (or open your page in a browser of your choice). You should see that the message "**Hello from the head**" appears. Then, as soon as you press the "**OK**" button, the message "**Hello from the Body**" should appear.

Well done, you have written your first piece of JavaScript code!

While this code consisted of very simple instructions to display a message onscreen, it shows how you can add some JavaScript code into your web pages.

So, now that we have written our first script, the next sections will look at how JavaScript programs are structured.

INTRODUCTION TO JAVASCRIPT SYNTAX

With JavaScript, you are communicating with the browser asking it to perform actions and using a language or a set of words bound by a syntax that the browser and you know. This language consists of keywords, key phrases, and a syntax that ensures that the instructions are understood properly. In computer science, these instructions need to be exact, precise, unambiguous, and with a correct syntax. In other words, it needs to be exact.

A syntax consists of a set of rules to be followed when writing your code. In the next section, we will learn how to use the proper syntax for JavaScript by combining the following:

- Statements.
- Comments.
- Variables.
- Operators.
- Assignments.
- Data types.
- Functions.
- Objects.
- Events.
- Comparisons.
- Type conversions.
- Reserved words.
- Messages to the console windows.
- Declarations.
- Calls to functions.

The list may look a bit intimidating but, not to worry, we will explore these in the next sections, and you will get to know and use them smoothly.

STATEMENTS

When you write a piece of code, as we have done in the HTML files that you have just created, you need to tell the system to execute your instructions (e.g., to print information) using statements. A statement is literally an order or something that you ask the system to do. For example, in the next line of code, the statement will tell the browser to display a message using an alert window:

```
alert("Hello Word");
```

When writing statements, there are a few rules that you need to know:

- Order of statements: in a script, each statement is executed sequentially in order of appearance. For example, in the next example, the code will display **hello**, then **word;** this is because the associated statements appear in that order in the script.

```
alert("hello");
alert("world");
```

- Statements are separated by **semi-colons** (i.e., semi-colon at the end of each statement). This is not required all the time (e.g., end of a line), but it is good practice to follow this rule for consistency and clarity.

> Note that several statements can be added on the same line, as long as they are separated by a semi-colon.

- For example, the next line of code has a correct syntax.

```
alert("hello");alert ("world");
```

- Multiple spaces are ignored for statements; however, it is good practice to add spaces around the operators such as +, -, /, or % for clarity. For example, in the next example, we state that **a** is equal to **b**. There is a space both before and after the operator =.

```
a = b;
```

- Statements to be executed together (e.g., based on the same condition) can be grouped using what is usually referred to as **code blocks**. In JavaScript, code blocks are symbolized by curly brackets (e.g., { or }). So, in other words, if you needed to group several statements, we would include them all within the same curly brackets, as follows:

```
{
    alert ("hello stranger!");
    alert ("today, we will learn about scripting");
}
```

As we have seen earlier, a statement usually employs or starts with a keyword (i.e., a word that the computer knows). Each of these keywords has a specific purpose and the most common ones (at this stage) are used for:

- Displaying an alert box: the keyword is **alert**.

Introduction to Programming in JavaScript

- Printing a message in the console window: the keyword is **console.log**.

- Declaring a variable: the keyword is **var**.

- Declaring a function: the keyword is **function**.

- Marking a block of instructions to be executed based on a condition: the keywords are **if** and **else**.

- Exiting a function: the keyword is **return**.

Now that you know a bit more about statements, let's modify your initial scripts to include more statements:

- Please open the scrip **myFirstScript.html** in the editor of your choice.

- Add the following code (new code in bold):

```
<SCRIPT>
    alert("Hello from the head");
    {
        alert ("this is my first script");
        alert ("This statements and the previous one belong to the same block of instructions");
    }
</SCRIPT>
```

In the previous code:

- We have created a block of instructions that starts with an opening curly bracket and that ends with a closing curly bracket.

- Within this block, we have created two statements based on alert boxes; both statements are ending with a semi-colon.

You can now save your code and refresh the corresponding browser page; you should see two additional messages displayed on the screen (i.e., the ones that you have just added).

For now, using blocks of instructions may look like it will not make much of a difference to your coding, and this is true for now. This being said, blocks of instructions are very helpful, as we will see later, especially when we need to tell the browser to execute a list of instructions. This is because, in this case, instead of telling the browser to execute each instruction individually, we can instead, ask for a block of instructions to be executed.

COMMENTS

In JavaScript, you can use comments to explain the code and to make it more readable. This is important for you, as the size of your code increases, and it is also important if you work as part of a team, so that team members can understand your code and make amendments in the right places if and where necessary.

When code is commented, it is not executed and there are two ways to comment your code in JavaScript using **single** or **multi-line** comments.

In single-line comments, a **double forward slash** is added at the start of a line or after a statement, so that this line (or part thereof) is commented, as illustrated in the next code snippet.

```
//the next line displays hello onscreen
alert ("hello");
```

In multi-line comments, any text between /* and */ will be commented (and not executed). This is also refereed as **comment blocks**.

```
/* the next lines after the comments displays the message hello onscreen
we then display another message
*/
alert("Hello");
alert("Another message");
```

> In addition to providing explanations about your code, you can also use comments to prevent part of your code to be executed. This is very useful when you would like to debug your code and find where the error or bug might be, using a very simple method. By commenting sections of your code, and by using a process of elimination, you can usually find the issue quickly. For example, you can comment all the code and run the script; then comment half the code, and run the script. If it works without no errors, it means that the error is within the code that has been commented, and if it does not work, it means that the error is in the code that has not been commented. In the first case (when the code works), we could then just comment half of the portion of the code that has already been commented. So, by successively commenting more specific areas of our code, we can get to discover what part of the code includes the bug. This process is often called **dichotomy** (as we successively divide a code section into two).

Let's use comments in our script:

- Please open the script **myFirstScript.html** in the editor of your choice.

- Modify the code as follows (new code in bold).

Introduction to Programming in JavaScript

```
<!DOCTYPE html>
<HTML>
    <HEAD>
        <TITLE>My First HTML Page</TITLE>
        <SCRIPT>
            //alert("Hello from the head");
            {
                alert ("this is my first script");
                alert ("This statements and the previous one belong to the same block of instructions");
            }
        </SCRIPT>
    </HEAD>
<BODY>
        Hello World<BR>
        Click here for Google.
        <SCRIPT>
            //alert("Hello from the body");
        </SCRIPT>
    </BODY>
</HTML>
```

In the previous code, we comment the message **alert("Hello from the head")** and the message **alert("Hello from the body")**.

Now that you have made these changes, please save your code and refresh the corresponding page in your browser; you should see that, this time, only two messages are displayed on screen, because the two other messages (or statements) have been commented.

We could also use multi-line comments as follows (new code in bold).

```
<SCRIPT>
    //alert("Hello from the head");
    /*
    {
        alert ("this is my first script");
        alert ("This statements and the previous one belong to the same block of instructions");
    }
    */
</SCRIPT>
```

In the previous code, we used a multi-line comment. This means that the two lines comprised between /* and */, while they belong to the file, will not be executed.

If you save your code and refresh the corresponding web page, you should see that no message is displayed onscreen, because all the **alert** statements have been commented.

VARIABLES

Now that you know a bit more about statements and comments, we will start to learn more about variables, which are quite important in JavaScript, as you will probably use them in most of your programs to perform calculations or to work with text.

So what is a variable?

A variable is a container. It includes a value that may change over time. When using variables, we usually need to: (1) declare the variable, (2) assign a value to this variable, and (3) possibly combine this variable with other variables using operators.

Let's look at an example of how variables can be employed.

```
var myAge;//we declare the variable
myAge = 20;// we set the variable to 20
myAge = myAge + 1; //we add 1 to the variable myAge
```

In the previous example, we declare a variable called **myAge**, we set it to **20** and we then add **1** to it.

Note that in the previous code, we have assigned the value **myAge + 1** to the variable **myAge**. The = operator is an assignment operator; in other words, it is there to assign a value to a variable and is not to be understood in a strict algebraic sense (i.e., that the values or variables on both sides of the = sign are equal).

When using variables, there are a few things that we need to determine including their name, type and scope:

- **Name of a variable:** A variable is usually given a unique name so that it can be identified uniquely. The name of a variable is usually referred to as an identifier. When defining an identifier, it can, contain letters, digits, a minus, an underscore or a dollar sign, and it usually begins with a letter. Identifiers cannot be keywords (e.g., such as **if**).

- **Type of variable:** variables can hold several types of data including numbers (e.g., numbers with or without decimals), text (i.e., these are usually referred as strings), arrays, Boolean values (e.g., true or false), or objects (e.g., we will look at this concept later), as illustrated in the next code snippet.

```
var myName = "Patrick";//the text or string is declared using double quotes
var currentYear = 2015;//the year needs no decimals and is declared as an integer
var width = 100.45;//width is declared as a number with decimals
```

- **Variable declaration:** a variable needs to be declared before its and the declaration is performed using the keyword **var**. At the declaration stage, the variable does not have to be assigned a value, as this can be done later. The next code snippet illustrates a variable declaration.

```
var myName;
myName = "My Name"
```

In the previous example, we declare a variable called **myName** and it is then assigned the value **"My Name"**.

- **Scope of a variable:** a variable can be accessed (i.e., referred to) in specific contexts that depend on where in the script the variable was declared. We will look at this concept later.

Common variable types include:

- **Strings**: same as text.

- **Numbers without decimals**: these are integers (e.g., 1, 2, 3, etc.).

- **Numbers with decimals**: for example, 1.2, 1.3, etc.

- **Boolean variables**: for example, true or false.

- **Objects**: these are structures that include several attributes (i.e., properties) and associated functions (i.e., methods).

- **Arrays**: a collection of variables of objects of the same type.

Note that it is possible to declare several variables in the same statement, as follows:

```
var name="Pat", location = "Ireland", year = 2018;
```

So let's experiment with variables using our script:

- Please open the script **myFirstScript.html**.

- Add the following code to it (new code in bold)

```
<HEAD>
    <TITLE>My First HTML Page</TITLE>
    <SCRIPT>
        var myName = "Patrick";
        alert ("Hello " + myName);
        //alert("Hello from the head");
        /*
        {
            alert ("this is my first script");
            alert ("This statements and the previous one belong to the same block of instructions");
        }
        */
    </SCRIPT>
</HEAD>
```

In the previous code:

- We declare a variable called **myName**.

- It becomes a string as we assign the word **Patrick** (surrounded by double quotes) to this variable.

- We then use the **alert** keyword to display a message that starts with **"Hello"** followed by the content of the variable **myName**.

> Note that if we had omitted the quotes around the word **"Patrick"**, the browser would have assumed that we referred to a variable called **Patrick** as opposed to a string for which the content is **"Patrick"**. Using the latter would have caused an error. We will come back to this later and see how it is possible to locate an error in your scripts.

OPERATORS

Once we have declared and assigned a value to a variable, we can use operators to modify or combine this variable with other variables. There are different types of operators available in JavaScript, including arithmetic operators, assignment operators, comparison operators and logical operators.

So let's look at each of these.

- **Arithmetic operators** are used to perform arithmetic operations including additions, subtractions, multiplications, or divisions. Common arithmetic operators include +, -, *, /, or % (modulo) and their use is illustrated in the next code snippet.

```
var number1 = 1;// the variable number1 is declared
var number2 = 1;// the variable number2 is declared
var sum = number1 + number2;// adding two numbers and store them in sum
var sub = number1 - number2;// subtracting two numbers and store them in sub
```

- **Assignment operators** can be used to assign a value to a variable and include =, +=, -=, *=, /= or %= and their use is illustrated in the next code snippet.

```
var number1 = 1;
var number2 = 1;
number1+=1; //same as number1 = number1 + 1;
number1-=1; //same as number1 = number1 - 1;
number1*=1; //same as number1 = number1 * 1;
number1/=1; //same as number1 = number1 / 1;
number1%=1; //same as number1 = number1 % 1;
```

Note that the = operator, when used with strings, will concatenate them (i.e., add them one after the other to create a new string). When used with a number and a string, the same will apply and the result is a string (for example "**Hello**"+1 will result in "**Hello1**").

- **Comparison operators** are often used for conditions to compare two values. Comparison operators include ==, !=, >, <, >= and >= and their use is illustrated in the next code snippet.

```
if (number1 == number2); //if number1 equals number2
if (number1 != number2); //if number1 and number2 have different values
if (number1 > number2); //if number1 is greater than number2
if (number1 >= number2); //if number1 is greater than or equal to number2
if (number1 < number2); //if number1 is less than number2
if (number1 <= number2); //if number1 is less than or equal to number2
```

Let's use some of these operators in your own code:

- Please open the script **myFirstScript.html**.
- Add the following code to it (new code in bold).

```
<SCRIPT>
    var myName = "Patrick";
    alert ("Hello " + myName);
    var yearOfBirth = 1990;
    var age = 2018-yearOfBirth;
    alert ("You are " + age + " years old");
```

In the previous code:

- We declare the variables **yearOfBirth** and **age**.
- We subtract the year of birth from the current year.
- The result of this subtraction is saved in the variable called **age.**
- We display the result.

CONDITIONAL STATEMENTS

While we have looked at simple variables such as numbers or text, and how to modify them through operators, we will now look at conditional statements.

Conditional statements are statements that are performed based on a condition, hence their name. Their syntax is usually as follows:

```
if (condition) statement;
```

This means **if the condition is verified (or true) then (and only then) the statement is executed**. When we assess a condition, we test whether a declaration (or statement) is true.

For example, by typing **if (a == b)**, we mean "**if it is true that a equals b**". Similarly, if we type **if (a>=b)** we mean "**if it is true that a equals or is greater than b**"

As we will see later, we can also combine conditions. For example, we can decide to perform a statement if two (or more) conditions are true. For example, by typing **if (a == b && c == 2)** we mean "**if a equals b and c equals 2**". In this case using the operator **&&** means AND, and that both conditions will need to be true. We could compare this to making a decision on whether we will go sailing tomorrow.

For example, we could translate the sentence "**if the weather is sunny and the wind speed is less than 5km/h then I will go sailing**" as follows.

```
if (weatherIsSunny == true && windSpeed < 5) IGoSailing = true;
```

When creating conditions, as for most natural languages, we can use the operator **OR** noted ||. Taking the previous example, we could translate the following sentence "**if the weather is too hot or the wind is faster than 5km/h then I will not go sailing** " as follows.

```
if (weatherIsTooHot == true || windSpeed >5) IGoSailing = false;
```

Another example could be as follows.

```
if (myName == "Patrick") alert("Hello Patrick");
else alert ("Hello Stranger");
```

In the previous code, we display the text "**Hello Patrick**" if the variable **myName** equals to "**Patrick**"; otherwise, we display the message "**Hello Stranger**".

> When we assess true and false conditions, we are effectively applying what is called **Boolean logic**. Boolean logic deals with Boolean numbers that have two values 1 and 0 (or true and false). By evaluating conditions, we are effectively processing Boolean numbers and applying Boolean logic. While you don't need to know about Boolean logic in depth, some operators for Boolean logic are important, including the **! operator**. It means **NOT** or "**the opposite of**". This means that if a variable is true, its opposite will be false, and vice versa. For example, if we consider the variable **weatherIsGood = true**, the value of **!weatherIsGood** will be **false** (its opposite). So the condition **if (weatherIdGood == false)** could also be written **if (!weatherIsGood)** which would literally translate as "if the weather is **NOT** good".

Let's experiment with conditional statements:

- Please open the script **myFirstScript.html**.

- Add the following code (new code in bold) at the beginning of the script:

```
<TITLE>My First HTML Page</TITLE>
<SCRIPT>
      var nameOfUser = prompt("Please  enter your name","");
      if (nameOfUser == "Patrick") alert ("Hello Patrick");
      else alert ("Hello Stranger");
```

In the previous code:

- We declare the variable **nameOfUser**.

- We then ask (or "prompt") the user to enter his or her name using the **prompt** method, which is a method provided by JavaScript. The first parameter is the label of the box (i.e., "**Please enter your name)**" and the second parameter, which is an empty string at present, defines the text that will be displayed as the default answer. Once the name has been entered by the user, it is stored in the variable **nameOfUser**.

- We then execute a conditional statement based on the value of the variable **nameOfUser**. If the text entered is "**Patrick**" (note that this is case-sensitive, so the browser is looking for this exact string, accounting for the case of each letter within), then the message "**Hello Patrick**" is displayed. Otherwise, the message "**Hello Stranger**" is displayed.

You can now save your code and refresh the corresponding web browser page, and you should see the following box:

Introduction to Programming in JavaScript

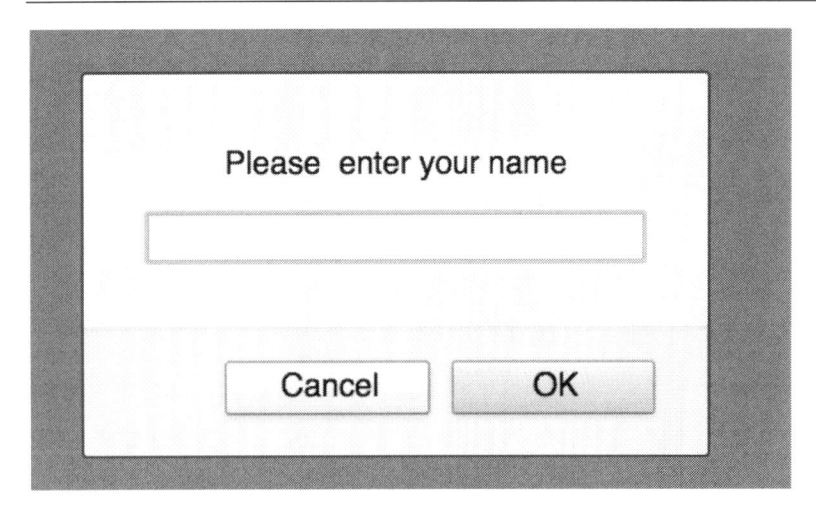

Figure 1-2: Using the Prompt function

- As you enter the name **"Patrick"** and press the button labelled "**OK**", the following message should appear.

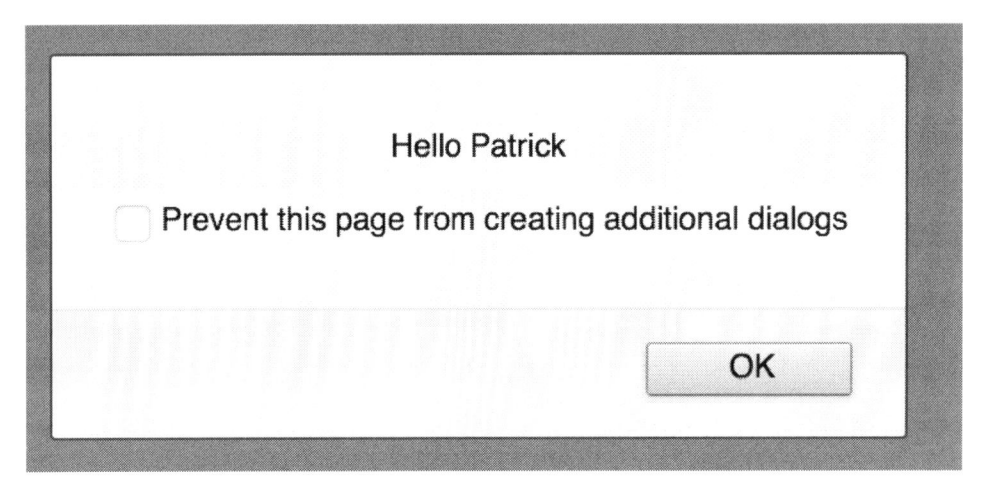

Figure 1-3: Displaying a message based on the user input

- You can then click on the button labeled "**OK**".

Now that we have used conditional statements for strings, we can also experiment with numbers. So, please amend the code in your you HTML file (new code in bold).

```
<TITLE>My First HTML Page</TITLE>
<SCRIPT>
    /*var nameOfUser = prompt("Please  enter your name","");
    if (nameOfUser == "Patrick") alert ("Hello Patrick");
    else alert ("Hello Stranger");*/

    var result = prompt("What is 1 + 1","");
    if (result == "2") alert ("Well done");
    else alert ("Sorry, wrong answer");
```

In the previous code:

- We comment the previous code.

- We declare a variable called **result**.

- We then ask (or "prompt") the user to enter his/her guess using the **prompt** method. The first parameter is the label of the box and the second parameter which is an empty string at present, defines the text that will be displayed as a default answer. Once the answer has been entered, it is stored in the variable **result**.

- We then perform a conditional statement based on the value of the variable **result**. If the text entered is "2", then the message "**Well done**" is displayed, otherwise, the message "**Sorry Wrong Answer**" is displayed instead.

Note that in the previous example, we ask for a number to be entered; however, because it is entered in a prompt box, it will be considered as a string by JavaScript. This is the reason why we are using double quotes around the number "2" when testing the answer; ideally, and we will look into this later, we could have converted the entry to a number and the code could have looked like as follows:

```
var result = prompt("What is 1 + 1","");
resultAsNumber = parseInt(result);
//if (result == "2") alert ("Well done");
if (resultAsNumber == 2) alert ("Well done");
else alert ("Sorry, wrong answer");
```

In the previous code:

- We declare the variable **resultAsANumber**.

- We convert the answer provided by the user, which is a string so far, to an integer (i.e., a number with no decimals).

- This new number is then stored in the variable called **resultAsANumber**.

- The conditional statement now uses the number **2** as a condition as opposed to the string "**2**".

Note that if you want to copy/paste the code from this book, make sure that the double quotes are straight and not curled, otherwise, the browsers may perceive the curled quotes as an error.

You can now save your code and refresh the corresponding web browser page and you should see, as for the previous example, a prompt asking you to enter a number.

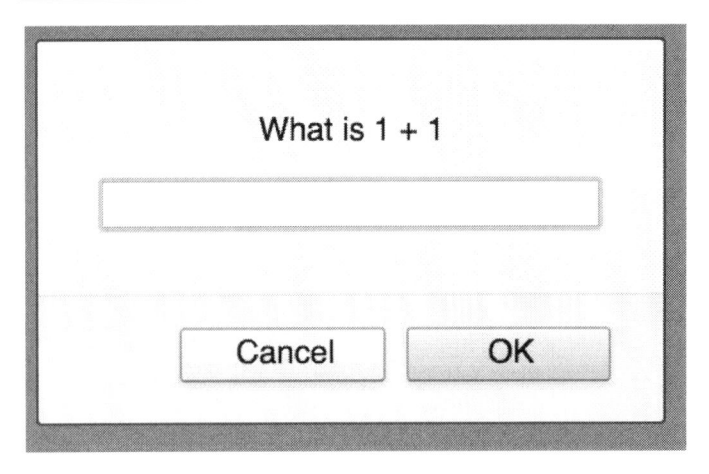

Figure 1-4: Asking the user to enter a number

- After entering the number **2** and pressing the "**OK**" button, the following message should appear.

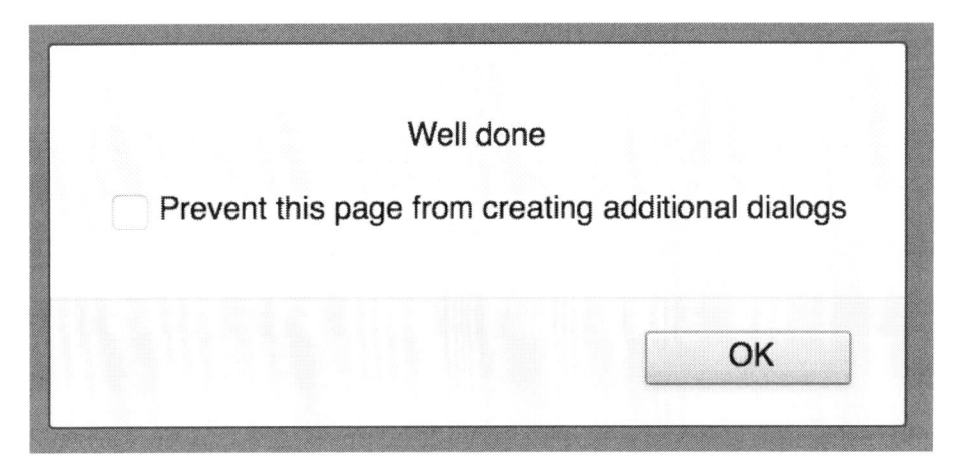

Figure 1-5: Displaying feedback

FUNCTIONS

Now that you can declare and combine numbers and strings, it is a good time to start looking into functions.

Functions can be compared to a friend or a colleague to whom you gently ask to perform a task, based on specific instructions, and to return information afterwards, if need be.

For example, you could ask your friend the following: "**Can you please tell me when I will be celebrating my 20th birthday given that I was born in 2000**". So you give your friend (who is good at Math :-)) the information (i.e., the date of birth) and s/he will calculate the year of your 20th birthday and give this information back to you. So in other words, your friend will be given an input (i.e., the date of birth) and s/he will return an output (i.e., the year of your 20th birthday). Functions work exactly this way: they are given information (and sometimes not), perform an action, and then sometimes, if needed, return information.

In programming terms, a function is a block of instructions that performs a set of actions. It is executed when invoked (or put more simply **called**) from the script, or when an event occurs (e.g., when the player has clicked on a button; we will see more about events in the next section). As for variables, functions are declared and can also be called.

Functions are very useful because once the code for a function has been created, it can be called several times without the need to rewrite the same code all over again. Also, because functions can take parameters, a function can process these parameters and produce or return information accordingly; in other words, they can perform different actions and produce different outputs based on the input. As a result, functions can do one or all of the following:

- Perform an action.
- Return a result.
- Take parameters and process them.

A function is declared using the keyword **function**, as follows**:**

```
function nameOfTheFunction ()
{
    Perform actions here
}
```

In the previous code the function does not take any input; neither does it return an output. It just performs actions.

```
function nameOfTheFunction (parameterName)
{
    Perform actions here
    return value;
}
```

In the previous code the function takes a parameter (i.e., an input), performs actions, and then returns a value. In this example, the parameter that is passed will be referred as **parameterName** within the function.

Introduction to Programming in JavaScript

A function can be called using the () operator, as illustrated in the next code snippet:

```
nameOfTheFunction1();
nameOfTheFunction2(value);
var test = nameOfFunction3(value);
```

In the previous code, a function is called with no parameter (first line), or with a parameter (second line). On the third line, a variable called **test** will be set with the value returned by the function **nameOfFunction3**.

Let's experiment with functions and create our very own function:

- Please open your HTML file and comment your previous code as follows:

```
/*var result = prompt("What is 1 + 1","");
resultAsNumber = parseInt(result);
//if (result == "2") alert ("Well done");
if (resultAsNumber == 2) alert ("Well done");
else alert ("Sorry, wrong answer");          */
```

- Then add the following code within the **SCRIPT** tags located in the head of the document:

```
<SCRIPT>
    var myAge = calculateAge (1990);
    alert ("My Age is " + myAge);

    function calculateAge(yearOfBirth)
    {
            return(2018-yearOfBirth);
    }
```

In the previous code:

- We declare a variable called **myAge**.

- We call the function **calculateAge**, passing the number **1990** as a parameter.

- The information (or value) returned by the function is stored in the variable **myAge** and then displayed using the **alert** function.

- The function **calculateAge** is declared; it takes one parameter called **yearOfBirth**. So any parameter passed to this function will be referred as **yearOfBirth** within this function.

- This function returns the result of the subtraction **2018 – yearOfBirth**.

- When the function is called, **yearOfBirth** is equal to **1990**; so it will return **28** (i.e., **2018-1990**).

Please save your code, and refresh the corresponding web page, and you should see the following message.

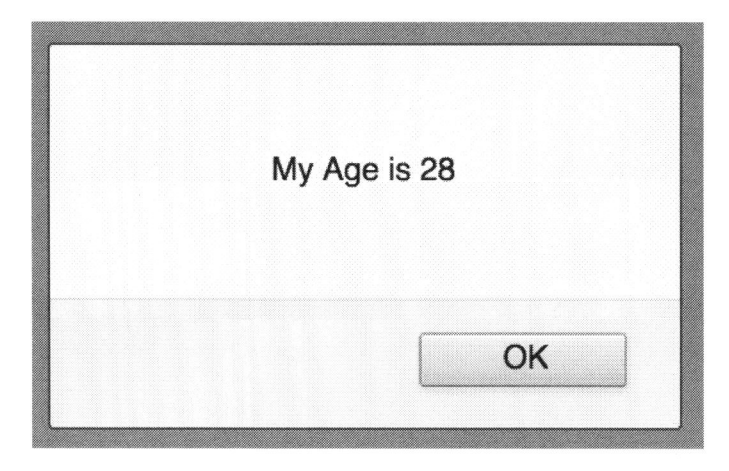

Figure 1-6: Displaying the value returned by the function

SCOPE OF VARIABLES

Whenever you create variables in JavaScript, you will need to be aware of their scope so that you use it where its scope makes it possible for you to do so. This is particularly important if you use functions, as some variables will be used just locally, whereas others will be used throughout the script.

The scope of a variable refers to where you can use this variable in a script. In JavaScript, variables can be either **global** or **local**.

> You can compare the terms **local** and **global** variables to a language that is either local or global. In the first case, the local language will only be used (i.e., spoken) by the locals, whereas the global language will be used (i.e., spoken) and understood by anyone whether they are locals or part of the global community.

- Global variables can be used anywhere in your script, hence the name **global**. These variables need to be declared at the start of the script (using the usual declaration syntax) and outside of any function. They can then be used anywhere in the script, as illustrated in the next code snippet.

```
var myVar;
function function1()
{
    myVar = 0;
}
function function2()
{
    myVar = myVar + 1;
}
```

In the previous code, the global variable **myVar** is declared at the start of the script; it is then initialized in **function1**, and updated in **function2**.

- Local variables are declared (and should only be used) within a specific function; hence the term local, because they can only be used locally, as illustrated in the next code snippet.

```
function function1()
{
    var myVar:int;
    myVar = 0;
}
function function2()
{
    var myVar2:int;
    myVar2 = 2;
}
```

In the previous code, **myVar** is a local variable to the function **function1**, and can only be used within this function; **myVar2** is a local variable to the function **function2**, and can only be used within this function.

If a variable is initialized in a method without being declared, it is considered as a global variable, as illustrated in the next code snippet.

```
function function3()
{
     testGlobal = 3;
}
function3();
alert("value of test" + testGlobal);//this should display "value of test 3";
```

In the previous code, the variable **testGlobal** has not been defined using the **var** keyword, and it is therefore **global** and accessible throughout the script (i.e., inside and outside the function **function3**)

Note that it is always good to avoid what is called variable masking/shadowing, which occurs when you give a local variable the same name as a global variable in the same file, as this could lead to confusions.

So let's experiment with variables and their scope:

- Please add the following code to the beginning of the SCRIPT area in the head of the document **myFirstScript.html**.

```
var myGlobalVariable = 3;
myFunction();
alert ("The value of myLocalVariableFromMyFunction is"+myLocalVariableFromMyFunction);
function myFunction()
{
     alert ("The value of myGlobalVariable is"+myGlobalVariable);
     var myLocalVariableFromMyFunction = 4;
}
```

In the previous code:

- We declare a global variable called **myGlobalVariable**; because it is declared outside any function, this variable will be global and accessible throughout our script.

- We then call the function **myFunction**.

- In the function called **myFunction**, we display the value of the variable **myGlobalVariable** and we also declare a local variable called **myLocalVariableFromFunction** and set it to **4**.

- Finally, we try to display the value of the local variable **myLocalVariableFromFunction** from outside the function where it was first defined. Since this is a local variable, this should not be possible, and hence, this should trigger an error.

Please save your code and refresh the corresponding web browser page. You should see that the browser displays the value of the variable **myGlobalVariable**; however, nothing happens after this message. That is, the value of the global variable is not displayed onscreen. As you may have guessed, this is normal because we are trying to display the value of the local variable **myLocalVariableFromFunction** from outside the function where it was first defined. Since this is a local variable, this should not be possible, and hence, it should trigger an error.

In JavaScript, a script will be executed until an error occurs in this script, and this is exactly what has happened here; this being said, it would be great to see errors and possibly where they originate from, to be able to, if need be, detect and correct bugs in our code. Thankfully, errors are usually displayed in what is called the **console** window of your browser, and we will learn more about this window, in the next section.

USING THE CONSOLE WINDOW

The console window is usually provided in most modern browsers and it makes it possible to display errors or messages that you can write from your code, essentially for debugging purposes. While in most browsers the console window can be accessed using the **F12** key, it can also be accessed as follows:

- In **Internet Explorer**: Select **Tools | Developer Tools | Console**.

- In **FireFox**: Install the plugin called FireBug (http://getfirebug.com) and then select **Tools | WebDevelpper | Web Console**.

- In **Safari**: Install Firebug Lite (http://safari-extensions.apple.com) and then select **Tools | WebDevelopper | Web Console**.

Once you have activated the console window in your browser, it should appear at the bottom of the browser window, and look like the following figure:

Figure 1-7: Using the console window

If your refresh the page that we have created so far (i.e., **myFirstScrpit.html**) and select the **Console** tab located at the bottom of the window, you should see the following messages in the console window.

Figure 1-8: Reading error messages in the console window

This message means that the variable **myLocalVariableFromFunction** is not defined; this is because, as we have seen before, we are trying to access a variable outside its scope, that is, from outside the function **myFunction** where it was previously defined as a local variable.

You may also see, to the right of this message, some information about the location of the error, as illustrated in the next figure:

myFirstScript.html:8:4

Figure 1-9: Displaying the location of the error

In the previous figure, the console window specifies that the error was detected in the file called **myFirstScript**, at the **line number 8 and row number 4**. If you look at the HTML file, this corresponds exactly to the line where we have tried to access a local variable from outside its function and scope, as illustrated in the next figure.

```
1   <!DOCTYPE html>
2   <HTML>
3       <HEAD>
4           <TITLE>My First HTML Page</TITLE>
5           <SCRIPT>
6               var myGlobalVariable = 3;
7               myFunction();
8               alert ("The value of myLocalVariableFromMyFunction is" myLocalVariableFromMyFunction);
9               function myFunction()
10              {
11
12                  alert ("The value of myGlobalVariable is"+myGlobalVariable);
```

Figure 1-10: Localizing errors and bugs

So as you can see, the console window is very useful to debug your code and to locate errors. This is very important because, when an error is detected, the browser will just stop to execute any further code, and it may be difficult to detect errors otherwise.

In addition to error messages, you can also display messages yourself in the console window, using the keyword **console.log**.

For example, the following code will display the sentence "**Starting Function1**" in the console window.

```
console.log ("Starting Function1")
```

After this short introduction to the console window, let's try to use this feature in our code:

- Please open the file **myFirstScript.html**.

- Modify the code as follows (new code in bold):

```
var myGlobalVariable = 3;
myFunction();
console.log("Trying to access the local Variable");
alert ("The value of myLocalVariableFromMyFunction is"+myLocalVariableFromMyFunction);
console.log("Managed To Access the the local Variable ")
```

In the previous code we have added two messages to the console window. As you save and display the web page in your browser, you should see an alert box. After pressing the **OK** button from the alert box, you should also see one additional message in the console window, as illustrated in the next figure.

```
 Inspector    Console    Debugger    { } Style Editor    Performance

 Filter output

    Trying to access the local Variable
 ▲▶ ReferenceError: myLocalVariableFromMyFunction is not defined  [Learn More]
```

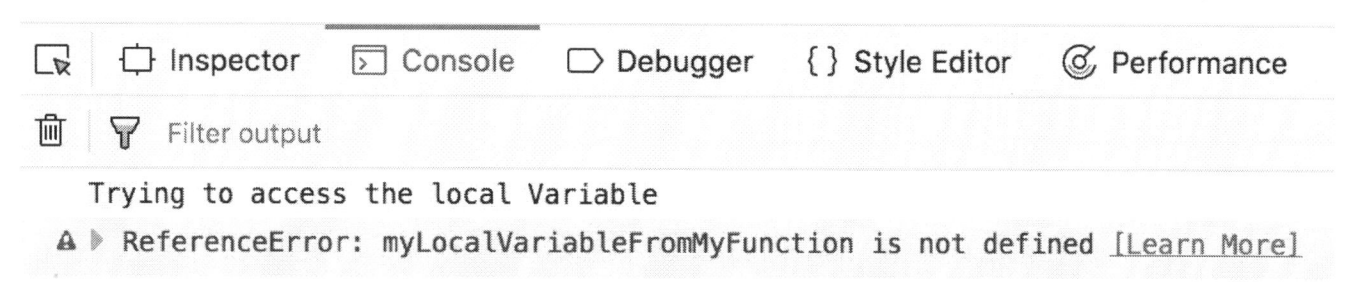

Figure 1-11: Displaying messages in the Console window

As you can see, only the first console message was displayed (i.e., "Trying to access the local Variable"); this is because the next line creates an error; therefore, the next part of the code, including the second message, is not executed by the browser.

STORING ALL SCRIPTS IN ONE FILE

Often, your JavaScript code will be stored in an HTML file; however, you can also use external JavaScript files to store all your scripts; this provides several advantages, including:

- All your scripts are stored in one place.
- You can avoid the duplication of your scripts and code, and hence save time coding.
- Your code is neater and easier to read and maintain.

So let's say that you have created three functions that will be used throughout your pages, and that you would like these to be available in only one place, you could do the following:

- Create a file called, for example, **myFunctions.js**, with a content similar to the following:

```
function add()
{

}
function test()
{

}
```

You could then use these in a different HTML file as follows:

```
<HTML>
    <HEAD>
        <SCRIPT src = "./myScript.js"></SCRIPT>
    </HEAD>
</HTML>
```

In the previous code we specify that some of our code is stored in a file called **myScript.js** that is located in the same folder as the current HTML page.

A FEW THINGS TO REMEMBER WHEN YOU CREATE A SCRIPT (CHECKLIST)

When you start coding, you will, as for any new activity, make small mistakes, learn what they are, improve your coding, and ultimately get better at writing your scripts. As I have seen in the past with students learning scripting, there are some common errors that are usually made; these don't make you a bad programmer; on the contrary, it is part of the learning process because *we all learn by trial and error, and making mistakes is part of the learning process*.

So, as you create your first script, set any fear aside, try to experiment, be curious, and get to learn the language. It is like learning a new foreign language: when someone from a foreign country understands your first sentences, you feel so empowered! So, it will be the same with JavaScript, and to ease the learning process, I have included a few tips and things to keep in mind when writing your scripts, so that you progress even faster. You don't need to know all of these by now (I will refer to these later on, in the next chapter), but it is so that you are aware of it and also use this list if any error occurs. So, watch out for these: :-)

- Each opening bracket has a corresponding closing bracket.

- All variables are written consistently (e.g., spelling and case). The name of each variable is case-sensitive; this means that if you declare a variable **myvariable** but then refer to it as **myVariable** later on in the code, this may trigger an error, as the variable **myVariable** and **myvariable**, because they have a different case (upper-case **V**), are seen as two different variables.

- As much as possible, declare a variable prior to using it (e.g., **var myVar**).

- For each variable name, all words (except for the first word) have a capitalized initial. This is not a strict requirement, however, it will make your code more readable.

- For each function, all words (except for the first word) have a capitalized initial. This is not a strict requirement; however, it will make your code more readable.

- All statements are ended with a semi-colon. This is not a strict requirement; however, it will make your code more readable.

- For **if** statements the condition is within round brackets.

- For **if** statements the condition uses the syntax "==" rather than "=".

- When calling a function, the exact name of this function (i.e., case-sensitive) is used.

- When referring to a variable, it is done with regards to the scope of the variable (e.g., call local variables locally).

- Local variables are declared and can be used within the same function.

- Global variables are declared outside functions and can be used anywhere within a script.

COMMON ERRORS AND BEST PRACTICES

As you will start your journey through JavaScript coding, you may sometimes find it difficult to interpret the errors produced by the browser. However, after some practice, you will manage to recognize them, to understand (and also avoid) them, and to fix them accordingly. The next list identifies the errors that my students often come across when they start coding in JavaScript.

When your script contains an error, the browser usually provides you with enough information to check where it has occurred, so that you can fix it. While many bugs are relatively obvious to spot, some others are trickier to find. In the following, I have listed some of the most common errors that you will come across as you start with JavaScript.

The trick is to recognize the error message so that you can understand what the browser is trying to tell you. Again, this is part of the learning process, and you **WILL** make these mistakes; however, the more you see these errors, and the more you will learn to understand them (and avoid them too :-)).

Again, the browser is trying to help you by communicating, to the best that it can, where the issue is. By understanding the error messages, we can get to fix them easily.

The browser usually provides the following information when an error occurs:

- The name of the script where the error was found.

- The row and column where the error was found.

- A description of the error.

As we will see in the next sections, error messages are displayed in the console window. The console window is a usually provided in most modern browsers and makes it possible to locate errors. In most browsers, the console window can be accessed using the **F12** key.

On the following figure, you can see that the browser indicates that an error has occurred. The message says **"Assets/Scripts/myFirstScript.js (23,34) BCE0085: Unknown identifier: 'localVariable'"**. So the browser is telling us that an error has occurred in the script called **myFirstScript**, at the line **23**, and around the **34th** character (i.e., column) on this line. In this message, it is telling us that it can't recognize the variable **localVariable**.

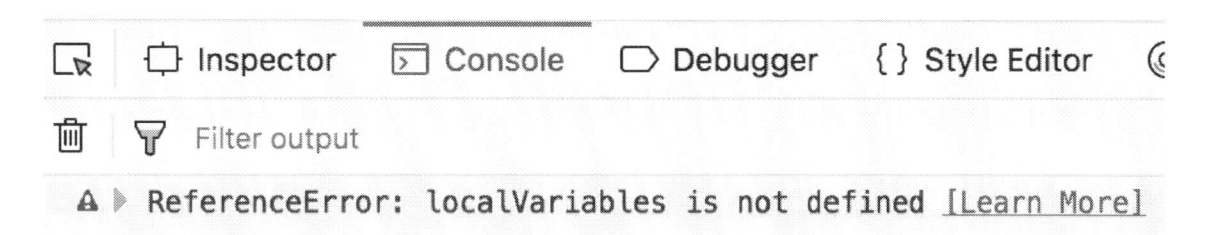

Figure 1-12: Interpreting errors

Introduction to Programming in JavaScript

To ensure that your code is easy to understand and that it does not generate countless headaches when trying to locate errors, there are a few good practices that you can start applying as you start coding; these should save you some time along the line by avoiding obvious errors.

Variable naming

- Use meaningful names that you can understand, especially after leaving your code for two weeks.

```
var myName = "Patrick";//GOOD
var b = "Patrick";//NOT SO GOOD
```

- Capitalize the initial of all words in the name, except for the first word.

```
var testIfTheNameIsCorrect = true;// GOOD
var testifthenameiscorrect = true; // NOT SO GOOD
```

Functions

- Use unique (i.e., different) names (for global and local variables).

- Check that all opening brackets have a corresponding closing bracket.

- Indent your code.

- Comment your code as much as possible to explain how it works.

LEVEL ROUNDUP

SUMMARY

In this chapter, we have managed to create your very first scripts. You have become more comfortable with the creation of variables and functions, as well as the display of information through the console window or alert boxes. Finally, you also learned how to employ conditional statements so that processing can be performed based on specific conditions. Building on this knowledge, you created simple programs where the user enters information and where the program computes and outputs a result accordingly. So we have covered some significant ground here from no knowledge of JavaScript to creating your first script: well done!

Quiz

It is now time to test your knowledge. Please specify whether the following statements are TRUE or FALSE. The answers are available on the next page.

1. JavaScript code is usually included with the tags <SCRIPT> and </SCRIPT>.
2. JavaScript code can only be added to the head of an HTML document.
3. JavaScript code can only be added to the body of an HTML document.
4. The command **alert** displays information in the *Console* window.
5. The command **console.log** displays information in the *Console* window.
6. In JavaScript, text values are surrounded by double quotes.
7. In JavaScript a local variable can only be used in the function where it was initially defined.
8. In JavaScript a global variable can be used throughout the script where it was declared.
9. In JavaScript a function always returns a value.
10. In JavaScript a code that is commented is not executed.

Solutions to the Quiz

1. TRUE.
2. FALSE.
3. FALSE.
4. FALSE (it is a pop-up window).
5. TRUE.
6. TRUE.
7. TRUE.
8. TRUE.
9. FALSE.
10. TRUE.

Checklist

You can move to the next chapter if you can do the following:

- Create variables.
- Combine variables.
- Create a function.
- Call a function.

Challenge 1

Now that you have managed to complete this chapter and that you have gathered interesting skills, let's put these to the test. This particular challenge will get you to become more comfortable with functions. The solutions are included in the resource pack.

Create a function called **calculatePrice** that does the following:

- Take two parameters called **nbItems** and **unitPrice**.
- Multiply these two numbers and store the result in a variable called **finalPrice**.
- Return the value of the variable **finalPrice**.

Once the function has been created, call this function using two values of your choice and display the result returned by the function in the console window.

Challenge 2

Create a function that does the following:

- Prompt the user for his/her first name.
- Prompt the user for his/her first last name.
- Display the full name (i.e., first name followed by a space, followed by the last name) using an alert box.

Once the function has been created , call this function.

2
OBJECTS & STRUCTURES

In this section you will discover how to work with customized structures, such as loops, and conditional statements, to optimize your code.

After completing this chapter, you will be able to:

- Know about objects and prototypes.

- Create and use constructors.

- Create an arrays to optimize your code.

- Store (and loop through) elements of an array.

- Understand how loops and arrays can be combined.

- Use and manipulate dates using their built-in methods and properties.

- Use and manipulate strings and numbers through JavaScript's built-in methods and properties.

Objects & Structures

WORKING WITH STRING VARIABLES

In the previous sections, we have learned how to declare and to manipulate variables such as numbers, and strings. As we have seen earlier, it is possible to perform simple operations such as additions or concatenations on strings. However, as we will see in this section, JavaScript also offers useful built-in functions and attributes that make it possible to perform subtler operations on strings. While there are over 20 built-in string functions in JavaScript, we will focus, in this section, on some of the most useful and commonly employed functions and attributes to manipulate strings.

So, let's look at some of these.

As we will see later, strings are considered as objects (put simply, a variable that includes a collection of other variables and functions), with associated attributes (often called properties) and functions (often referred as methods). These attributes and methods are accessible using what is called the dot notation, that is, by adding a dot after the name of the string, as we will see in the next examples.

So let's look at some attributes for string variables.

length: Length is an attribute that is available for all string variables and that provides the length of a string, which is the number of characters that it contains, as illustrated in the next code snippet.

```
var myName = "Patrick";
var numberOfLetters = myName.length;
console.log("There are " + numberOfLetters + " letters in " +myName);
```

In the previous code:

- We declare a string variable called **myName**.

- We then declare a new variable called **numberOfLetters** in which we will store the length of the string **myName**.

- We then display a message with the length of the string **myName**.

> Note that to access an attribute of a string, we use the **dot notation**, that is the name of the string followed by a dot followed by the name of the attribute that we are looking for. This notation can be interpreted as the word "of" and it can be read from right to left. So, for example, **myString.length** could be interpreted as the value <u>of</u> the attribute **Length** <u>of</u> the variable **myString**.

indexOf: this method returns the position where a character first appears in a string; it is useful when you would like to know if a string includes a specific character, and where this character is located within, as illustrated in the next code snippet.

```
var mySentence = "A sentence with the word Hello";
if (mySentence.indexOf("Hello") >=0 ) console.log ("Hello is part of the sentence");
else console.log ("Hello is not included in the sentence");
if (mySentence.indexOf("Hi") >=0 ) console.log ("Hi is part of the sentence);
else console.log ("Hi is not included in the sentence");
```

In the previous code:

Objects & Structures

- We declare a new string called **mySentence**.

- We check whether the word **Hello** appears in the sentence; since the first letter of the sentence starts at the index **0**, we know that if the word **Hello** appears from the index **0** onwards, that it is included in the sentence (since the index 0 referrers to the start of the sentence); if that's the case, we display a message accordingly.

- We also check whether the word **Hi** appears in the sentence; since the first letter of the sentence starts at the index 0, we know that if the word **Hi** appears from the index 0 onwards, that it is included in the sentence.

- If that's the case, we display a message accordingly.

You can now test this code, by opening the file **myFirstScript.html** (you can also create a new file if you wish), and by adding the previous code in the **SCRIPT** tags that are located in the **HEAD** section of your document; you can comment any previous code beforehand.

Please save your code and refresh the corresponding web page; you should see the following messages in the console window.

```
Hello is part of the sentence
Hi is not included in the sentence
```

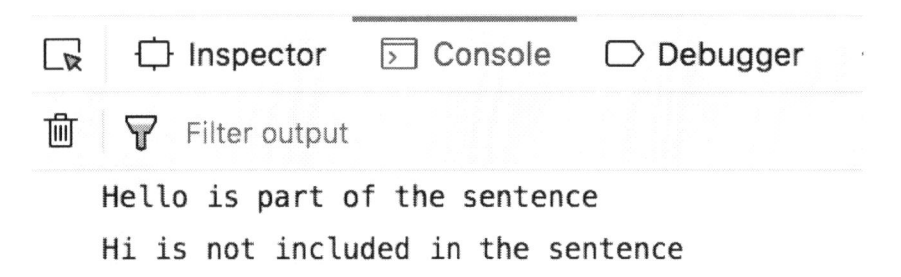

Figure 2-1: using the function indexOf

slice: In addition to locating a string within a string, JavaScript also makes it possible to remove (or to slice) part of a string, and this can be performed using the function **slice**, as illustrated in the next code snippet.

```
var mySentence = "This sentence is long and needs to be shorter";
var shorterSentence = mySentence.slice (0,14);
console.log(shorterSentence);
```

In the previous code:

- We declare a new string variable called **mySentence**.

- We then slice (or remove part of) this sentence starting at the first character (i.e., from the index 0) and ending at (and including) the 15th character (at the index 14).

- We then display the content of the slice.

> You can add the above code to your HTML file and see the result in the console window after refreshing the corresponding page in your browser.

replace: Sometimes, it can be very useful to replace characters within a string, and this can be done by just looking for a string within a sentence or paragraph, or by changing the case of string in a sentence. This technique is useful when you are collecting information from a form, for example, to ensure that some characters or words do not remain in the string entered by the user, or when you would like all the words in a sentence to be lower- or upper-case. The next code snippet illustrates how this can be done.

```
var mySentence = "This sentence is long and needs to be shorter";
var modifiedSentence = mySentence.replace ("is long","is way too long");
var upperCaseSentence = mySentence.toUpperCase();
var lowerCaseSentence = mySentence.toLowerCase();
```

In the previous code:

- We create a string called **mySentence**.

- We then replace the words "**is long**" by the words "**is way too long**" using the function **replace**, and we then save the result in the variable called **modifiedSentence**.

- In the next lines we successively convert all the letters in the variable **mySentence** to upper-case (using the function **toUpperCase**) or to lower-case (using the function **toLowerCase**).

We could test these functions ourselves, by doing the following:

- Open the script **myFirstScript.html** in your code editor.

- Comment the previous code as follows.

```
/*
var myGlobalVariable = 3;
myFunction();
console.log("Trying to access the local Variable");
alert ("The value of myLocalVariableFromMyFunction is"+myLocalVariableFromMyFunction);
console.log("Managed To Access the local Variable ")
function myFunction()
{
        alert ("The value of myGlobalVariable is"+myGlobalVariable);
        var myLocalVariableFromMyFunction = 4;
}

var myAge = calculateAge (1990);
alert ("My Age is " + myAge);

function calculateAge(yearOfBirth)
{
            return(2018-yearOfBirth);
}
*/
```

- Add the following code within the same **SCRIPT** tags.

Objects & Structures

```
<SCRIPT>
        var mySentence = "This sentence is long and needs to be shorter";
        var shorterSentence = mySentence.slice (0,14);
        console.log(shorterSentence);
        var modifiedSentence = mySentence.replace ("is long","is way too long");
        console.log(modifiedSentence);
        var upperCaseSentence = mySentence.toUpperCase();
        console.log("Upper Case: "+upperCaseSentence);
        var lowerCaseSentence = mySentence.toLowerCase();
        console.log("Lower Case: "+lowerCaseSentence);
```

In the previous code, as we have described earlier, we perform several operations on the string called **mySentence** and we then display the result in the console window.

- Please save the code, refresh the corresponding web browser page, and you should see the following messages in the console window:

```
This sentence
This sentence is way too long and needs to be shorter
Upper Case: THIS SENTENCE IS LONG AND NEEDS TO BE SHORTER
Lower Case: this sentence is long and needs to be shorter
```

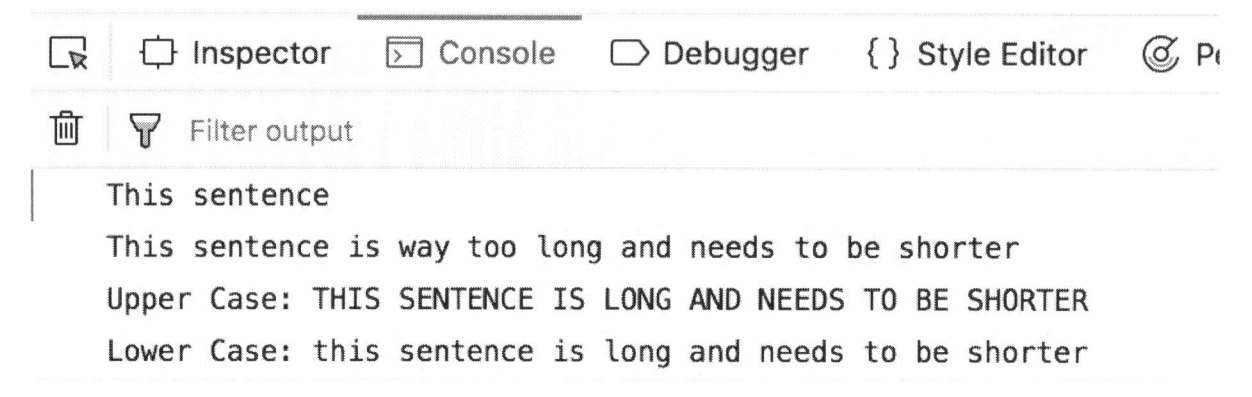

Figure 2-2: manipulating strings

While we have covered some of the most common string functions here, you can see the full list of JavaScript functions on the official website:

https://developer.mozilla.org/en-US/docs/Web/JavaScript/Reference/Global_Objects/String

WORKING WITH NUMBER VARIABLES

As you can see, built-in functions can be very useful when it comes to working with strings. Thankfully, built-in functions also exist for numbers so that they can be manipulated accordingly, sometimes through Mathematical calculations.

So, let's look at some very useful built-in attributes and function that can be used with numbers.

These attributes (or properties) and functions (i.e., methods) can help to convert between different types of variables, as follows:

- **toString**: this method converts a number to a string.
- **Number**: this method converts a variable (e.g., a string, a Boolean or a date) to a number.
- **parseInt**: this method converts a string to an integer (i.e., a number with no decimals).
- **parseFloat**: this method converts a string to a float (i.e., to a number with decimals).

JavaScript also includes methods that make it possible to perform advanced mathematical calculations, including:

- **Math.random**: returns a number between 0 and 1.
- **Math.pow (x,y)**: returns the value of x to the power of y.
- **Math.ceil (x)**: returns the value of x rounded-up to its nearest integer.
- **Math.floor (x)**: returns the value of x rounded-down to its nearest integer.
- **Math.sin (x)**: returns the sine of the angle x.
- **Math.min (x, y, z, ...)**: returns the lowest number in the list of arguments.
- **Math.max (x, y, z, ...)**: returns the highest number in the list of arguments.
- **Math.random()**: returns a random number comprised between 0 and 1, excluding 1.

Let's experiment with some of these:

- Please open the script **myFirstScript.html**.
- Comment the previous code.
- Add the following code within the **SCRIPT** tags:

Objects & Structures

```
var randomNmber = Math.random();
if (randomNmber <.7) console.log ("there was a 70% chance for this message to be displayed");
else console.log ("there was a 30% chance for this message to be displayed");
```

In the previous code:

- We generate a random number between 0 and 1 through the function **Math.random**, and we store the result in the variable called **randomNumber**.

- We then test whether this random number is less than **0.7**.

- In both cases (i.e., whether it is greater than or less than .7) we display a message in the console window accordingly.

Please save your code and refresh the corresponding page. You should see a message displayed in the console window for which the content will vary depending on the random number generated.

Again, we have only looked at common functions here; for a list of all the math functions you can look at the official documentation:

https://developer.mozilla.org/en-US/docs/Web/JavaScript/Reference/Global_Objects/Math.

Switch Statements

If you have understood the concept of conditional statements in the previous sections, then this section should be pretty much straight forward. Switch statements are a variation on the if/else statements that we have seen earlier. The idea behind the switch statements is that, depending on the value of a specific variable, we will switch to a portion of the code and perform one or several actions accordingly. The variable considered for the switch structure is usually a **number**. Let's look at a simple example:

```
var choice = 1;
switch (choice)
{
    case 1:
        console.log ("you chose 1");
        break;
    case 2:
        console.log ("you chose 2");
        break;
    case 3:
        console.log ("you chose 3");
        break;
    default:
        console.log ("Default option");
        break;
}
console.log ("We have exited the switch structure");
```

In the previous code:

- We declare the variable called **choice**, as an **integer** and initialize it to **1**.

- We then create a **switch** structure whereby, depending on the value of the variable **choice**, the program will switch to the relevant section (i.e., the portion of code starting with **case 1:**, **case 2:**, etc.). Note that in our code, we look for the values **1**, **2** or **3**. However, if the variable **choice** is not equal to 1 or 2 or 3, the program will go to the section called **default**. This is because this section is executed if none of the other possible conditions (i.e., choice=1, choice=2, or choice=3) have been fulfilled.

Note that each choice or branch starts with the keyword **case** and ends with the keyword **break**. The **break** keyword is there to specify that after executing the commands included in the branch (or the current choice), the program should exit the switch structure. Without any break statement, we will remain in the switch structure and the next line of code will be executed.

So let's consider the previous example and see how this would work in practice. In our case, the variable **choice** is set to **1**, so we will enter the **switch** structure, and then look for the section that deals with a value of **1** for the variable **choice**. This will be the section that starts with **case 1:**. Then the command **console.log ("you chose 1");** will be executed, followed by the command **break**, indicating that we should exit the switch structure; finally the command **console.log ("We have exited the switch structure")** will be executed.

Objects & Structures

Switch structures are very useful to structure your code and when dealing with mutually exclusive choices (i.e., only one of the choices can be selected) based on an integer value, especially in the case of menus. In addition, switch structures make for cleaner and easily understandable code.

So, let's experiment with the switch structure:

- Please open the file **myFirstScript.html**.

- Comment any previous code present in the **SCRIPT** tags embedded in the head of the file.

- Add the following code:

```javascript
var answer = prompt("Please enter your choice 1- 3","");
var choice = Number(answer);
switch (choice)
{
        case 1:
                console.log ("you chose 1");
                break;
        case 2:
                console.log ("you chose 2");
                break;
        case 3:
                console.log ("you chose 3");
                break;
        default:
                console.log ("Default option");
                break;
}
console.log ("We have exited the switch structure");
```

In the previous code:

- We ask the user to enter a choice between 1 and 3.

- We convert this choice to a number.

- We then display a corresponding message using a switch structure.

- After exiting the switch structure, we display another message.

You can now save your code and refresh the corresponding web browser page, and you should see the following prompt:

Objects & Structures

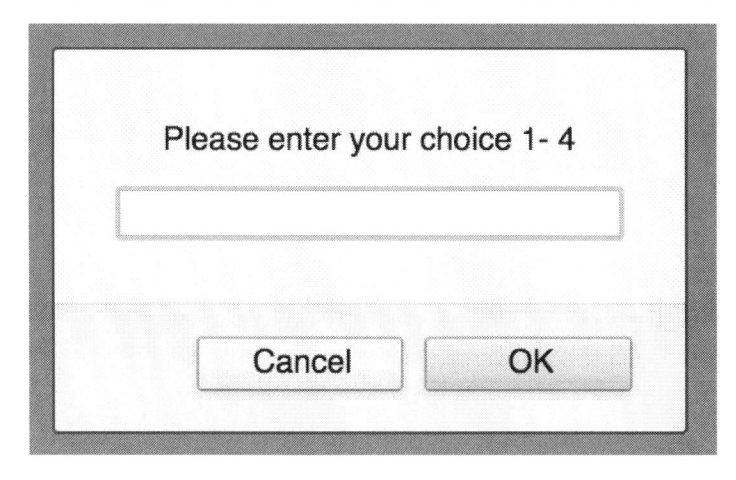

Figure 2-3: Asking for a number

Once you enter a number and press the **OK** button, a message similar to the following should be displayed in the console window.

```
you chose 3
We have exited the switch structure
```

Figure 2-4: Displaying the choice in the console window

51

Objects & Structures

LOOPS

There are times when you have to perform repetitive tasks as a programmer; many times, these can be fast-forwarded using loops which are structures that will perform the same actions repetitively based on a condition. So, the process is usually as follows when using loops:

- Start the loop.

- Perform actions.

- Check for a condition.

- Exit the loop if the condition is fulfilled or keep looping otherwise.

Sometimes the condition is tested at the start of the loop, some other times it is tested at the end of the loop. As we will see in the next paragraph, this will be the case for the **while** and **do-while** loop structures, respectively.

Let's look at the following example that is using a **while** loop.

```
var counter = 0;
while (counter <=10)
{
    counter++;
}
```

In the previous code:

- We declare the variable called **counter** and set its value to **0**.

- We then create a loop that starts with the keyword **while** and for which the content (which is what is to be executed while we are looping) is delimited by opening and closing curly brackets.

- We set the condition to remain in this loop (i.e., **counter <=10**). So we will remain in this loop as long as the variable counter is less than or equal to 10.

- Within the loop, we increase the value of the variable **counter** by **1**.

So effectively:

- The first time we go through the loop: the variable **counter** is increased to **1**; we reach the end of the loop; we go back to the start of the loop and check if the variable **counter** is less or equal to **10**; this is true in this case because **counter** equals 1.

- The second time we go through the loop: the variable **counter** is increased to **2**; we reach the end of the loop; we go back to the start of the loop and check if the variable **counter** is less or equal to 10; this is true in this case because **counter** equals **2**.

- …

- The 11th time we go through the loop: the variable **counter** is increased to **11**; we reach the end of the loop; we go back to the start of the loop and check if the variable **counter** is less or equal to 10; this is now false as **counter** now equals **11**. As a result, we exit the loop.

So, as you can see, using a loop, we have managed to increment the value of the variable **counter** iteratively, from 0 to 11, but using less code than would be needed otherwise.

Now, we could create a slightly modified version of this loop, using a **do-while** loop structure instead, as illustrated in the next example:

```
var counter = 0;
do
{
    counter++;
} while (counter <=10);
```

In the previous example, you may spot two differences, compared to the previous code:

- The **while** keyword is now at the end of the loop. So the condition will be tested (or assessed) at the end of the loop.

- A **do** keyword is now featured at the start of the loop.

So here, we execute statements first and then check for the condition at the end of the loop.

Another variation of the code could be as follows:

```
for (counter = 0; counter <=10; counter ++)
{
    console.log ("Counter = " + counter);
}
```

In the previous code:

- We declare a loop in a slightly different way: we state that we will use an integer variable called **counter** that will go from 0 to 10.

- This variable **counter** will be incremented by **1** every time we go through the loop.

- We remain in the loop as long as the variable **counter** is less than or equal to 10.

- The test for the condition, in this case, is performed at the start of the loop.

Loops are very useful to perform repetitive actions for a finite number of objects, or to perform what is usually referred as recursive actions. For example, you could use loops to go through an array of 100 items. So using loops will definitely save you some code and time when you use them.

So we could use a loop structure to improve the previous code that we have written so that the user is prompted to enter a number but also so that that we keep asking for a number as long as the choice is less than 1 or greater than 3, or if the data entered is not a number.

So let's just do that:

- Please open the script **myFirstScript.html**.

Objects & Structures

- Modify the script as follows (new code in bold):

```
do
{
        var answer = prompt("Please enter your choice 1- 3","");
        var choice = Number(answer);
} while (choice < 1 || choice >3);

switch (choice)
{
```

In the previous code:

- We create a **do-while** loop.

- Within the loop, we create a variable called **answer** based on the user's choice, as well as the variable **choice** which is the variable **answer** converted to a number using JavaScript's built-in function **Number**.

- We loop as long as the number entered is less than 1 or greater that 3.

ARRAYS

In the previous sections, we have learnt how useful loops and conditional statements can be. This being said, there are times when you may want to store similar types of information in a way that can be easily accessible and usable; for example, you may want to create a quiz and store all the questions and answers in a way that makes it easy to check if an answer is correct. In this case, an array can save you a lot of time. So let's look at arrays and see how they can be employed in JavaScript.

You can optimize your code with arrays, as they make it easier to apply features and similar behaviors to a wide range of data. When you use arrays, you can manage to declare less variables (for variables storing the same type of information) and to also access them more easily.

You can create either *single-dimensional* arrays or *multi-dimensional* arrays.

Let's look at the simplest form of arrays: **single-dimensional arrays**. For this concept, we can take the analogy of a group of 10 people who all have a name. If we wanted to store this information using a string variable, we would need to declare (and to set) ten different variables, as illustrated in the next code snippet.

```
var name1 = "Patrick";var name2 = "John"; var name3 = "Mary" ...
```

While this code is perfectly fine, it would be great to store this information in only one variable instead. For this purpose, we could use an array. An array is comparable to a list of items that we can access using an index. This index usually starts at 0 for the first element in the array.

So let's see how we could store the previous names with an array.

- We could declare and initialize the array as follows:

```
var names = new Array();
```

In the previous code, we define an array called **names**.

- We could then store information in this array as described in the next code snippet.

```
names [0] = "Patrick";
names [1] = "John";
...
names [9] = "Mary";
```

In the previous code, we store the name **Patrick** as the first element in the array (remember the index starts at 0); we store the second element (with the index 1) as **John**, as well as the last element (with the index 9), **Mary**.

Objects & Structures

> Note that for an array of size **n, the index of the first element is 0** and **the index of the last element is n-1**. So for an array of size 10, the index for the first element is 0, and the index of the last element is 9 (i.e., 10-1).

If you were to use arrays of numbers, the process would be similar, as illustrated in the next code snippet.

```
var arrayOfInts; arrayOfInts [0] = 1;
```

Now, one of the cool things that you can do with arrays is that you can initialize your array in one line, saving you the headaches of writing 10 lines of code if you have 10 items in your array, as illustrated in the next example.

```
var names = ["Paul","Mary","John","Mark", "Eva","Pat","Sinead","Elma","Flaithri", "Eleanor"];
```

This is very handy, as you will see in the next sections, and this should definitely save you a lot of time coding.

To illustrate the concept of arrays, we could create a very simple quiz where the user is asked several questions, and his/her answers are compared to the correct answers.

- Please open the script **myFirstScript.html**.
- Comment the previous code within the **SCRIPT** tags.
- Add the following code within the **SCRIPT** tags.

```
var questions = ["What is 2+2", "What is 4+2", "What is 4+5"];
var correctAnswers = [4, 6, 9];
for (i = 0; i < 3; i ++)
{
    var answer = Number(prompt(questions[i],""));
    if (answer == correctAnswers[i]) alert("Well done!"); else alert ("Sorry wrong answer");
}
```

In the previous code:

- We declare an array called **questions**, and we define its content; it consists of three strings that relate to the questions of the quiz.

- We then define a new array called **correctAnswers** and we define its content; it consists of the three solutions to the quiz.

- We create a loop; the idea is to go through the three questions of the quiz, to collect the answers, and to check if they are correct.

- The first time we go through the loop **i = 0**; we use the string included in **question [0]** for the question; that is, the text "**what is 2 + 2**"; we then record the answer, convert it to a number, and save it in the variable called **answer**; following this, we compare the answer from the user to the correct answer, that is **corretAnswer[0]** (which is 6) and display a message accordingly.

56

You can now save your code, and refresh the corresponding page in your browser. You should see that if you enter the correct answer to the first question (i.e., 4), an alert box should display the text "**Well done!**', as illustrated in the next figures.

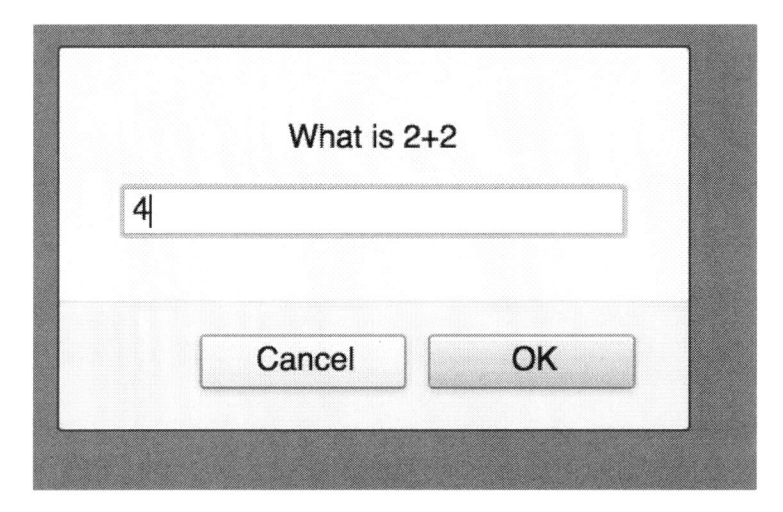

Figure 2-5: Entering the first answer

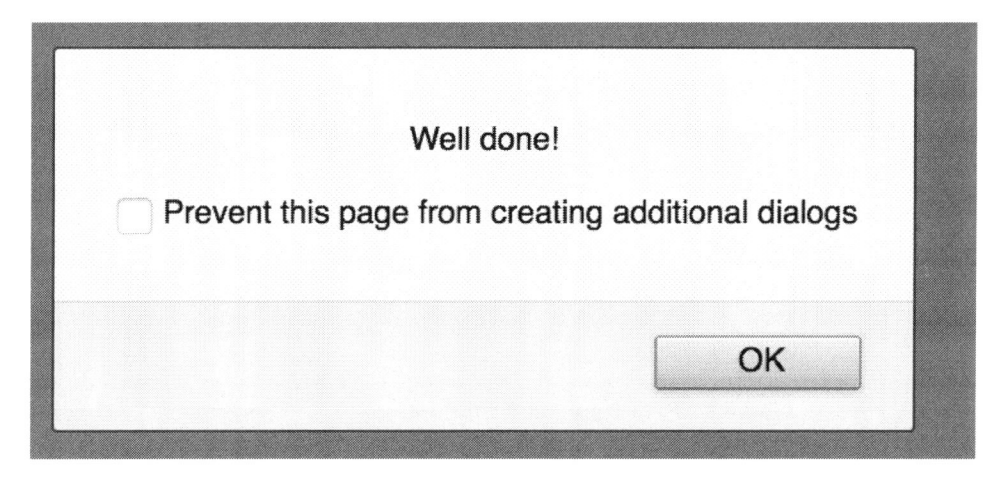

Figure 2-6: Displaying feedback

We could even jazz-up this quiz by adding the following:

- The question number.
- The total number of correct answers.
- The total number of incorrect answers.

So let's proceed with these changes.

- Please modify the code as follows (new code in bold):

Objects & Structures

```
var correctAnswers = [4, 6, 9];
var score = 0;
for (i = 0; i < 3; i ++)
{
    var answer = Number(prompt("Question "+ (i+1)+": "+questions[i],""));
    if (answer == correctAnswers[i])
    {
        alert("Well done!");
        score++;
    }
    else
    {
        alert ("Sorry wrong answer");
    }
}
alert ("You answered " + score + " questions correctly");
```

In the previous code:

- We declare a variable called **score** that will be used to track the score.

- When asking a new question to the user, we add the string **"Question"** followed by **i+1** to display the question number; so when **i = 0** we display the label **"Question 1"**, and so forth.

- Whenever a correct answer has been given, we increase the score by one.

- When all answers have been provided (i.e., when we are outside the loop) we display the number of correct questions.

You can now save your code and refresh the corresponding page; you should see that each question includes a label with the question number, as illustrated in the next figure.

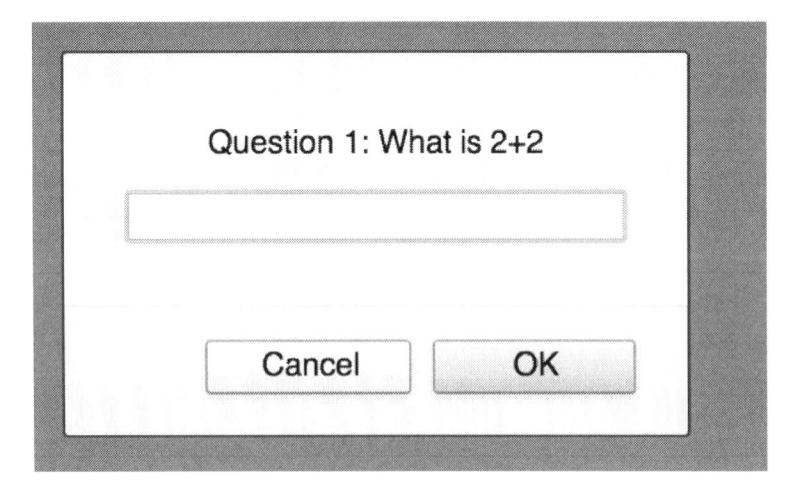

Figure 2-7: Adding a label to the questions

You should also see that the score is provided at the end of the quiz (i.e., after the last question has been answered).

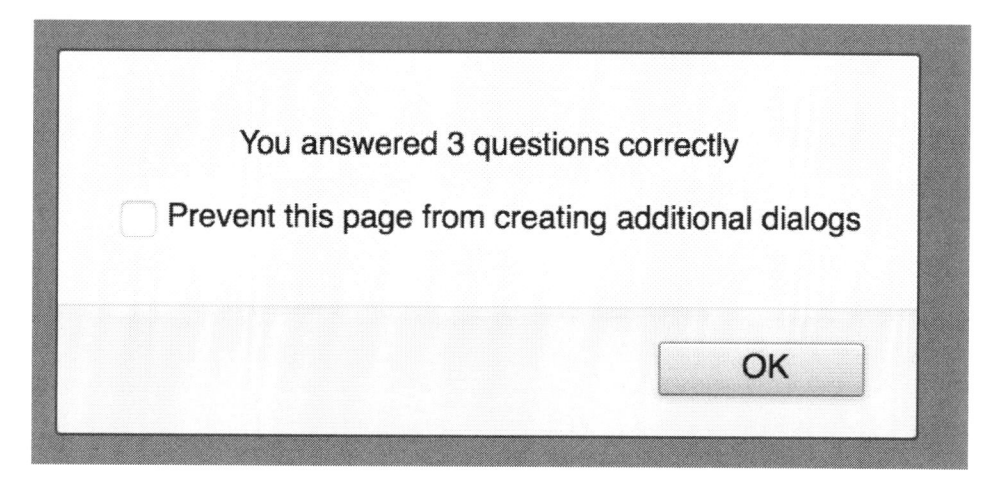

Figure 2-8: displaying the score

> One of the other interesting aspects of arrays is that, by using a loop, you can write a single line of code to access all the items in this array, and hence, write more efficient code.

Another interesting thing with arrays is that you can use built-in functions (i.e., methods) to manage your arrays and perform actions such as adding elements, removing elements, or even sorting the array.

Let's look at the **sort** function that is used in the next code snippet:

```
var test = ["Noemy", "Alan", "John"];
console.log("First Element before sort: " + test)
test.sort();
console.log("First Element after sort:" + test)
```

In the previous code:

- We declare an array made of three names, called **test**.

- We display the full array; by printing the array, all its elements are displayed, separated by a comma.

- We sort the array using the **sort** function.

- We print the array again and all its elements are displayed, separated by a comma, as illustrated in the next figure.

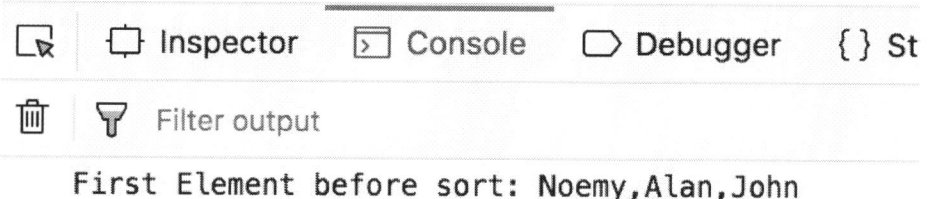

```
First Element before sort: Noemy,Alan,John
First Element after sort:Alan,John,Noemy
```

In our previous example, the elements of the array are sorted based on the first letter of each name. If this array included numbers instead, then they would have been sorted by increasing number, as per the next example.

Objects & Structures

```
var test = [4,6,8,5,7];
console.log("First Element before sort: " + test)
test.sort();
console.log("First Element after sort:" + test)
```

In the previous code, we create an array of numbers and we display its content before and after it has been sorted. The result is illustrated in the next figure.

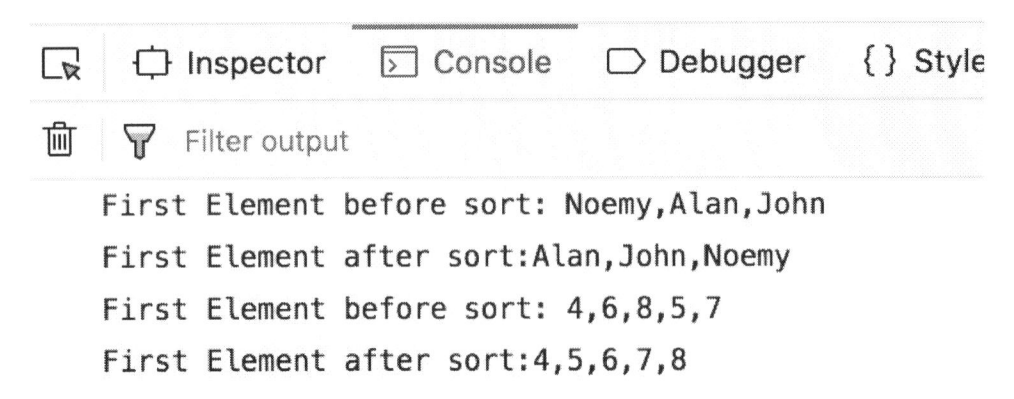

```
First Element before sort: Noemy,Alan,John
First Element after sort:Alan,John,Noemy
First Element before sort: 4,6,8,5,7
First Element after sort:4,5,6,7,8
```

For a full list of array functions, please consult Mozilla's official documentation here: **https://developer.mozilla.org/en-US/docs/Web/JavaScript/Guide/Indexed_collections#Array_object**.

WORKING WITH DATES

In JavaScript, you have the ability to create and manipulate dates; this can be useful when you would like, for example, to create a timer or a countdown. You may have seen countdowns on some web pages whereby the time remaining before an event is displayed and updated every seconds; another application is to know the weekday for a specific date (e.g., Monday, Tuesday, etc.).

JavaScript provides ways to create dates in different formats and to then obtain the corresponding seconds, minutes, or months also.

To start with date objects, let's look at how to create a date object; this can be done very simply as follows:

```javascript
var newDate = new Date();
```

In the previous code, we have just created a new variable of type date (to be exact it's an object of type **date**), that will store the current date; by default, if we don't specify any parameter when creating this object, the current date will be used. However, we could also create a date in the future for example, by specifying the year, month, or day as illustrated in the next code snippet.

```javascript
var deadline = new Date (2018, 05, 28, 23,59,59,0);
```

In the previous code:

- We specify a new date in the future.

- The first parameter defines the year.

- The second parameter defines the month; note that in this case, the first months of the year starts at the index 0, so we effectively specified the month of June.

- The third parameter defines the day of the month.

- The fourth parameter defines the hour (11pm).

- The fifth parameter defines the minute (59).

- The sixth parameter defines the seconds (59).

- And the last parameter defines the number of milliseconds.

Note that it is also possible to define a date based on the number of milliseconds and this is particularly helpful when you perform operations between dates and when you want to know how many seconds, or days are remaining until a specific date.

Objects & Structures

> It is good to bear in mind that when a new date object has been created, it is not updated automatically; so if we wanted to create a timer with the current date, we may need to use a function that updates this variable constantly, and we will have a look at this later.

So, let's see what we can do with date objects. Once a new date has been created you can manipulate or subtract dates; let's look at the following example:

```
todaysDate = new Date();
enDate = new Date (2018, 11, 24, 23,59,59,0);
var diff = Math.abs(enDate-todaysDate);
```

In the previous example:

- We create a date that corresponds to today (i.e., the current day).

- We also create a new date that corresponds to a specific deadline (i.e., Christmas!)

- We then calculate the number of milliseconds between these two dates and save the result in a variable called **diff**.

So at this stage we have the number of seconds between these two dates; what we would like to do is to calculate not only how many seconds we have to wait until Christmas, but also, so that it is easier to remember, how many days, hours and minutes until then.

To do so, we could calculate the number of days by dividing the number of milliseconds as follows:

```
var nbDays = Math.floor(diff/(1000*60*60*24));
```

In the previous code we obtain the number of days between the two dates by dividing the variable **diff** (number of seconds to Christmas), by 1000 (to obtain the number of seconds), then by 60 (to obtain the number of minutes), then by 60 (to obtain the number of hours) and by 24 (to obtain the number of days). We also use **Math.floor** to round-off the result.

The last thing we could do, would be to write the result in the console window as follows

```
console.log("NB Days left"+nbDays);
```

As you can see with the previous example, it is relatively easy to display a timer or the actual time; however, as you may have guessed, there can be a slight issue with this, in that the text displayed is not updated unless we call the function regularly; so if we wanted, for example, for this time to be updated every second, we may need to modify our code accordingly so that the function that displays the time is called every seconds; so we will see how this can be done in the next section.

First we need to calculate the number of minutes and seconds between the dates as follows:

- Please create a new HTML file and rename it, for example, dates.html.

- Add the usual **HEAD** and **BODY** sections to this document, as well as a **SCRIPT** section in the **HEAD** section.

Objects & Structures

- Please create the function **updateTimer** (new code in bold), in the SCRIPT section located in the HEAD of the document, as described in the next code snippet.

```
function updateTimer()
{
    var todaysDate = new Date();
    var enDate = new Date (2018, 11, 24, 23,59,59,0);
    var diff = Math.abs(enDate-todaysDate);
    var nbDays = Math.floor(diff/(1000*60*60*24));
    var nbHours = Math.floor(diff%(1000*60*60*24)/(1000*60*60));
    var nbMinutes = Math.floor(diff%(1000*60*60)/(1000*60));
    var nbSeconds = Math.floor(diff%(1000*60)/(1000));
}
```

In the previous code:

- We calculate the number of <u>full</u> days between the two dates by dividing the variable **diff** by 24 (24 hours in one day), then by 60 (60 minutes in one hour), by 60 (60 seconds in one minute), and 1000 (1000 milliseconds per seconds).

- The number of <u>full</u> hours left until the deadline is calculated by finding how many milliseconds are left in addition to the number of full days (**diff%(1000*60*60*24)**) and by then converting this number to hours by dividing it by **1000*60*60**.

- The number of <u>full</u> minutes left until the deadline is calculated, using the same technique, by finding how many milliseconds are left in addition to the number of full minutes (**diff%(1000*60*60)**) and by then converting this number to minutes by dividing it by **1000*60**.

- The number of <u>full</u> seconds left until the deadline is calculated, using the same technique, by finding how many milliseconds are left in addition to the number of full minutes (**diff%(1000*60)**) and by then by converting this number to seconds by dividing it by **1000**.

Then we could add the following code at the end of the function **updateTimer**.

```
document.getElementById("timer").innerHTML = nbDays+" Days";
document.getElementById("timer").innerHTML += nbHours+" Hours";
document.getElementById("timer").innerHTML += nbMinutes+" Minutes";
document.getElementById("timer").innerHTML += nbSeconds+" Seconds";
```

In the previous code, we insert the data calculated previously (i.e., number of days, hours, minutes, and seconds) in the corresponding DIV element (that we yet need to create). By using the operator **+=**, we add text to the text already present in the corresponding DIV element.

We can then create a placeholder to display the time by adding the following code to the body of the document.

```
<BODY onload="setInterval(updateTimer,1000);">
    <DIV id = "timer"> </DIV>
</BODY>
```

In the previous code:

- We specify that we should call the function **updateTimer** every 100 milliseconds (i.e., every second).

Objects & Structures

- We use the **onload** event for the body of the document so that the function **setInterval** is called just when the document has been loaded.

- The repeated call to the function **updateTimer** is performed through the function **setInterval** which includes two parameters: the name of the function to call and how often (in milliseconds) we'd like to call this function.

- We also create a div with the **ID** called timer so that the timer can be displayed.

> Note that the function **setInterval** is actually called a browser function, as we will see later; it can be written **window.setInterval** or **setInterval**. The reason why we can omit to use the word window is because we are, by default, working from the window object, which is the global object.

Also note that you can use two other window functions when dealing with timing as we have:

- **setTimeout**: to either call a function after a specific amount of time has elapsed.

- **clearTimeout**: to stop calling a function frequently, for example after you have specified how often it should be called with the function **setInterval**.

For more information on timing and associated functions, you can look at the official documentation here:

https://developer.mozilla.org/en-US/docs/Web/API/WindowOrWorkerGlobalScope/setInterval

OBJECTS

As we have seen in the previous sections, JavaScript makes it possible to store information in variables, often called primitives, such as numbers or strings, and this is very handy; however, there are times when you may like to describe the data that you are dealing with using more information; for example, you may think of storing the information about a student in one place, such has its id, first name, last name, and a list of the classes attended by this student. If we were to use the variable types that we have mentioned earlier, we would probably do this as follows.

- Please create a new HTML, named objects.html, for example file with the usual structure (i.e., a HEAD section, a BODY section, and a SCRIPT section within the HEAD).

- Include the following code in the SCRIPT section.

```
var firstName = "Paul";
var lastName = "Murphy";
var studentId = "ID101"
var classes = ['CS700', 'CS800'];
```

While the code above is fine, it would be great to group this information in a way that makes it easier to read and access later on; for this purpose, we could use an object that groups this information as follows:

- Please add the following line of code in the SCRIPT section.

```
var student1 = {fName: "Paul", lName: "Murphy", studentID:"ID101", classes: ['CS700', 'CS800']}
```

In the previous code:

- We have created what is called an object; the object is named **student1**.

- We then declare the variables (often called properties) that are included in this object.

- In our case, the object includes several properties such as **fName**, **lName**, **studentID**, and classes (which is an array of strings).

- Values are set for all these variables.

So you may wonder how it is possible to access these variables now; well, this is relatively simple: to access the member variables, we just need to use what is called the dot notation; in other words, this can be achieved by using the name of the object followed by a dot and then the name of the property that we want to access, as per the next example:

- Please add the following code to the SCRIPT section.

```
console.log("Student1: "+student1.fName);
```

In the previous example, we specify that we want to display the value of the property called **fName** for the object **student1**.

Objects & Structures

Now, as we have seen earlier, objects can include several variables, but they can also include methods (basically, functions); for example, we could define a method for the object called **student1** that displays the full name of the student; let's see how.

- Please modify the code as follows (new code in bold):

```
var student1 =
{
    fName: "Paul",
    lName: "Murphy",
    studentID:"ID101",
    classes: ['CS700', 'CS800'],
    displayName :
            function (){console.log("My name is " + this.fName + " "+this.lName);}

}
//console.log("Student1: "+student1.fName);
console.log(student1.displayName());
```

In the previous code, we define a method (i.e., a function for a specific object) called **displayName**. This method, when called, will write a message that includes the full name of the student in the console window.

You can now save your file, and open it in a browser window, you should see the message "**My Name is Paul Murphy**" in the console window.

Now, there are, in fact, other ways to create objects in JavaScript; the method that we have used to create our object called **student1** is called a **literal**, as we literally created the object on the spot along with its methods and properties; this being said, there are even more efficient uses of objects and ways to create them.

For example, let's say that you'd like to create several objects each for a specific student; in this case, you could duplicate the code that we have created earlier for **student1** and change it slightly to create a new object called **student2**; however, if you want to create 10 students, this will become quite time consuming, and instead, what we could do to be more efficient is to create a template for a typical student that includes all properties and methods within, and then reuse this template for each new student. This type of template can be created via **constructors**. So let's have a look at constructors.

CONSTRUCTORS

In JavaScript, a constructor will make it possible to create objects that have the same structure in terms of properties and methods. Let's take the example of students.

We could create a template for each student that includes information on their first name, their last name, their student ID and the courses that they attend. For this purpose, we could create a constructor as follows:

- Please add the following code to your HTML file (i.e., **objects.html**, if this is the name you have chosen previously).

```
function Student (firstName, lastName, studendIdentification, classesAttended)
{
            this.fName = firstName;
            this.lName = lastName;
            this.studentId = studendIdentification;
            this.classes = classesAttended;
}
```

In the previous code:

- We create a function called **Student**. This function will take four parameters that correspond to the student's first name, their last name, their ID and the classes attended.

- When called, this function will use the value of the parameters passed to set the corresponding properties for this object.

- We use the keyword **this** to specify that we are accessing the property called **fName** from the **current** object; the same applies to the properties **lName**, **studentId**, and **classes**.

Once the constructor has been created, we can then use it to create a new **Student** objects as follows:

- Please add the following code to your HTML file (i.e., **objects.html**, if this is the name you have chosen previously).

```
var student3 = new Student("David", "Callagher", "120",['CS700', 'CS800']);
console.log("Student3" + student3.lName);
console.log("Student3" + student3.classes[0]);
var student4 = new Student("Mary", "Black", "121,['CS701', 'CS800']);
console.log("Student4" + student4.lName);
console.log("Student4" + student4.classes[0]);
```

In the previous code:

- We declare the variable **student3** and set it by calling the **constructor** that we have created early-on.

- We pass four parameters to this constructor: A first name, a last name, a student ID, and the two courses for which the student is enrolled.

Objects & Structures

- We then display the last name of the student, followed by the first class that this student is enrolled in.

- We repeat the previous steps for a new student.

So, as you can see, constructors are very useful when creating several object that share similar properties or methods.

MODIFYING OBJECTS

Once an object has been created, it is possible to include additional properties and methods to it, in two ways: by adding these to the object itself or by adding these to the constructor.

Let's look at the next code snippet to see the first way to apply this feature:

- Please add the following code to your HTML file (i.e., **objects.html**, if this is the name you have chosen previously).

```
student3.fullName = student3.fName + " " + student3.lName;
console.log("Student 3's full name: "+student3.fullName);
```

In the previous code:

- We declare the property **fullName** for the object **student3**.

- We set this variable to be a combination of the **first** and the **last** name of the student.

- We then print the value of the property called **fullName** in the console window.

You can now refresh the corresponding page and see the additional message "**Student 3's full name: David Callagher**" in the console window.

While you can modify the property of an object that has been created, you can also modify the property of the actual constructor, so that all objects created from this constructor include the new property; this can be done as follows, by adding the following line of code to the **Student** constructor.

- Please add the following code to the Student constructor.

```
this.fullName = this.fName + " " + this.lName;
```

As we have seen in the previous section, you can add new properties to an existing object; you can also add a new method, using the same principle; for example, we could modify the constructor called **Student** to include a method that calculates the number of modules attended by this student; first we could modify the **Student** constructor by adding this line to it:

```
this.nbModulesAttended = function() {return this.classes.length;}
```

In the previous code, we create a new method for the constructor **Student**. This new method called **nbModulesAttended** will return the size of the array called **classes** for the **Student** object, which is effectively the number of classes attended.

We could then use the next line of code to access this method:

```
console.log("NB modules attended by Student 3: "+ student3.nbModulesAttended())
```

The same technique can be used to add a method to an object that has been created.

Objects & Structures

> Note that it is also possible to access an object's properties using the syntax: **objectname["property"]**. For example, **Student["fName"]**.

Level roundup

Summary

In this chapter, we have managed to create several structures to organize your code and data such as loops, conditional statements, arrays, objects and constructors. We also looked into built-in data types and their associated methods and properties to be able to manipulate numbers, strings, and dates. Finally, you also learnt how to combine loops and arrays to create a very simple quiz, and how to combine timing built-in functions, and dates to create a count-down. So we have covered some significant ground here from little knowledge of JavaScript to creating your first applications!

Objects & Structures

Quiz

It is now time to test your knowledge. Please specify whether the following statements are TRUE or FALSE. The answers are available on the next page.

1. The String method size will return the number of characters in a string.

2. The method **Math.ceil** will round-up a number to its nearest integer.

3. Switch statements can be compared to conditional statements.

4. The following code will create a new array.

```
var names = new Array();
```

5. The array method called **sort** will sort all the element of a specific array.

6. When subtracting two dates, the result of the subtraction is usually expressed in seconds.

7. The method **setTimeInterval** can be employed to call a specific function as regular intervals.

8. An object literal can include a method.

9. The same constructor can be used to create different objects.

10. It is possible to modify an object after it has been created.

Solutions to the Quiz

1. FALSE (its length).
2. TRUE.
3. TRUE.
4. TRUE.
5. TRUE.
6. FALSE (it's milliseconds).
7. FALSE (it's **setInterval**).
8. TRUE.
9. TRUE.
10. TRUE.

Objects & Structures

Checklist

You can move to the next chapter if you can do the following:

- Create objects.
- Define prototypes and create corresponding objects.
- Create Date object.
- Manipulate strings.

Challenge 1

Now that you have managed to complete this chapter and that you have gathered interesting skills, let's put these to the test. This particular challenge will get you to become more comfortable with objects and prototypes. The solutions are included in the resource pack.

- Create a constructor called **Car**.
- This constructor should take three parameters: the **make**, **model**, and **speed** of the car.
- Add the following properties to the constructor: **make**, **model**, **speed**.
- Add the following methods to the constructor: accelerate (increases the speed by one), decelerate (decreases the speed by one).
- When called the properties of the car will be set using the parameters passed to the constructor.
- Create a new object based on this constructor of type **Car** with the parameters of your choice.
- Call the accelerate method for this Car object and display the new speed in the console window.

Challenge 2

Create a quiz based on the code covered in this chapter with the following features

- Use arrays to store the questions and answers.
- The quiz will include 10 questions.
- The questions are related to the name of famous inventors.
- All answers need to be converted to lower case by the JavaScript code.

- The feedback is only provided at the end of the quiz, with the number correct answers.

Adding Interaction

3
ADDING INTERACTION

In this section we will discover how to add interaction to your web pages using JavaScript and concepts such as events, DOM, forms or event listeners.

After completing this chapter, you will be able to:

- Know how to use the Document Object Model (DOM).

- Know how to detect and process events on your page such as clicks.

- Know how to listen to several events for a given element.

- Know how to access elements in your page through JavaScript.

- Validate information entered by the user through forms.

- Use JavaScript's built-in form validation library.

- Remove or add elements to a web page using JavaScript.

PROCESSING EVENTS

Throughout this book and in JavaScript, you will read about events. Events can be compared to something that happens at a particular time, and when an event happens, something (e.g., an action) usually needs to be performed. For example, when your alarm goes off in the morning (event), you can either get-up (action) or decide to go back to sleep. When you receive an email (event), you can decide to read it (action), and then reply to the sender (another action). In programming terms, the concept of events is quite similar, although the events that we will be dealing with will be slightly different.

So, we could be looking for when a user clicks on some text (that's an event) and then display a message accordingly (that's an action), or wait until they press a button onscreen (that's another event) to perform some calculations (that's an action).

In JavaScript, a function is usually called whenever an event occurs. The function, in this case, is often referred as a handler, because it "handles" the event. You have then the opportunity to modify this function and to add instructions (i.e., statements) that should be followed when this event occurs.

Again, to use another analogy, we could write instructions to a friend on a piece of paper, so that, in case someone calls in our absence, the friend knows exactly what to do.

So a function, in this case, can be compared to the piece of paper with instructions, as it will include a set of statements to be executed in case a particular event occurs.

Sometimes information is passed to this function about the particular event, and sometimes not.

Common JavaScript events, include:

- Detecting when the page is loaded; the event is called **onload**.

- Detecting when the user has clicked on an element; the event is called **onclick**.

- Detecting when the user moves the mouse over an element; the event is called **onmouseover**.

- Detecting when the user moves the mouse away from an element; the event is called **onmouseout**.

- Detecting when the user has selected an element (e.g., clicked on a text field); the event is called **onfocus**.

- Detecting when the user has moved away from an element (e.g., tab on a text field); the event is called **onblur**.

> Note that a document includes a collection of nodes; nodes can be elements, whereby, an element is a node that is defined by tags and that have properties such as attributes or an id.

So let's experiment with some of these events.

- Please create a new HTML file with the usual structure and rename it **events.html** (or any other name of your choice).

Adding Interaction

- Modify the body tag as follows:

```
<BODY onload = "pageLoaded();">
```

In the previous code, we modify the opening BODY tag to indicate that when the event **onload** happens (i.e., when the page has been loaded), we should call the function **pageLoaded** that we will define shortly after.

Now, we just need to create the function **pageLoaded**.

- Please add the following function to the SCRIPT tag located in the head of the document.

```
function pageLoaded()
{
    alert("The page has been loaded");
}
```

In the previous code, we define the function called **pageLoaded**. When this function is called, it displays an alert box with the message "**The page has been loaded**".

Once you have made these changes, you can save your code, and open the page in a browser, and you should see an alert window similar to the following:

Figure 3-1: Detecting when a page has been loaded

Once you have checked that your code is working properly, we can experiment with the **onclick** event, which is triggered when the user clicks on an element within the page.

- Please open the page **events.html** in your text editor.

- Add the following function to the SCRIPT tag.

```
function clickButton()
{
    alert("You just clicked the button");
}
```

- Add the following code to the body of the document (new code in bold).

78

```
<BODY onload = "//pageLoaded();">
<BUTTON onclick = "clickButton(); type = "button"> Click Me</BUTTON>
```

In the previous code:

- We comment the code that is to be executed if the page is loaded.

- We create a button using the tags **<BUTTON>** and **</BUTTON>**.

- We then specify that when this button is pressed, that the function **clickButton** should be called.

After saving your code and refreshing the corresponding page, it should look as follows:

Figure 3-2: Adding a button

And after pressing the button, the following alert box should appear:

Figure 3-3: Handling clicks

As you have seen in the previous example, it is very easy to detect and to process simple events, as long as you have specified what event should be handled/processed, and the function that should be called in this case. Again, these are very useful in order to add interaction to your page and to process users' actions.

Another interesting application of events is for form validation, when users enter information that needs to be checked. For example, you may have a page with a text field requiring people to enter their name, and you may want to check the content of the field whenever the user leaves this field by either pressing the TAB key or by clicking somewhere else in the document. The event, in this case, could be **onblur**.

There are, of course many more events that can be used in JavaScript, and we will look at them in the next sections of this book.

Adding Interaction

ACCESSING HTML ELEMENTS FROM JAVASCRIPT

Throughout the past sections, we have managed to not only create code that include variables, functions, arrays, and loops, but to also code that is executed based on specific events such as a mouse click or when the page has been loaded. This being said, since users often provide information through a page or read information on the page, it would be great to make your HTML pages more interactive by checking or modifying some of the content within through JavaScript.

For example, you may want to create a JavaScript program that reads the information entered by the user in a text field and that displays a corresponding information on the page. While alert boxes are useful for testing purposes, they are limited in the sense that you are missing on a wide range of data input techniques offered by HTML5 such as input text, sliders, or drop-down menus. So in this section, we will learn how to read from and write information on the page, and to specifically use the elements that are often employed in forms for data collection, such as text fields.

So let's get started.

JavaScript makes it possible to access most of the elements present in your HTML, including those present in the BODY or the HEAD of the document. This access is often performed through what is called a *Document Object Model* (a.k.a. DOM). Basically, the DOM is a hierarchy of all the elements found on your page, and it provides a path and ways to access, modify, remove or add any element or node in your document.

One of the easiest ways to access elements on your page is by giving an ID to an element and then by using this ID to access the element. In this case, we can use the following syntax:

```
document.getElementById("nameOfTheId").innerHTML.
```

Let's look at the following example:

```
<!DOCTYPE html>
<HTML>
<HEAD>
    <SCRIPT>
        function readField ()
        {
            var text = document.getElementById("myText").innerHTML;
            console.log("Text found: "+ text);
        }
    </SCRIPT>
</HEAD>
<BODY onload = readField()>
    <DIV id = "myText"> Hello World</DIV>
</BODY>
</HTML>
```

In the previous code:

- We create a DIV with the ID **myText**; this DIV includes text within (i.e., **Hello World**).

- We also create a function called **readField** that stores and displays the content of the text that is within the DIV identified by the ID **myText**.

- To find the relevant DIV, we use the syntax **document.getElementById** as a way to say, "**within the document, please select the element with the ID myText**".

- When this DIV has been found, we extract one of its properties (i.e., its content) using the dot notation and the keyword **innerHTML**. So, all in all, this statement means "**The HTML code within the tags of the DIV with the ID myText that is within the document should be stored in the variable called text**".

- Finally, we use the event **onload** to specify that the function **readField** should be called only when the page has been loaded; this is to ensure that the DIV element has been created before JavaScript tries to access it.

> Note that the following technique could have been applied to modify other HTML elements such as text comprised with headings.

You can now create a new file called **dom.html** (or any other name of your choice), and include the previous code. As you save your code, and open the page in a web browser, you should see the message "**Text Found: Hello World**" in the console window. This means that using JavaScript, we have managed to access and to save the content included in a DIV that is within the document.

As we have seen in the previous example, JavaScript makes it possible to read nodes within the document; this being said, you can also, in addition to reading the content of a node, modify its content, or even better, add new nodes.

> Note that a document includes a collection of nodes; nodes can be elements, whereby, an element is a node that is defined by tags and that have properties such as attributes or an id.

Let's look at these features:

- Please open the file **dom.html**.

- Modify the script as follows (new cold in bold).

```
<SCRIPT>
    function readField ()
    {
        var text = document.getElementById("myText").innerHTML;
        console.log("Text found: "+ text);
        document.getElementById("myText").innerHTML = "Hello Stranger";
    }
</SCRIPT>
```

In the previous code, we modify the content of the DIV with the ID called **myText** and include a new message within.

- You can then modify the BODY of the document as follows (new code in bold):

Adding Interaction

```
<!-- <BODY onLoad = readField()> -->
<BODY>
      <DIV onclick = "readField()" id = "myText"> Hello World</DIV>
</BODY>
```

In the previous code, we comment the previous opening BODY tag so that the function **readField** is not called when the page loads, but instead when the text is clicked. We also specify that we will call the function **readField** whenever the user clicks within the DIV.

You can save your code and refresh the corresponding browser window. At first you will see a text saying "**Hello World**"; however, after clicking on this text, it should turn to "**Hello Stranger**".

USING JAVASCRIPT WITH FORMS (PART 1)

While the example that we have covered in the previous section applies to DIVs and other HTML tags (e.g., H1, P, etc.), there are times when you may want to use HTML forms to gather information from the user, and check or modify this information (e.g., the content of a text field) accordingly.

Let's take the example of a form where the users need to enter their name in a mandatory field (i.e., this field should not be left empty). We could write a short piece of JavaScript code that checks when the user has entered information and when s/he has left the field so that the content can be checked accordingly.

The following example illustrates how this can be done:

- Please add the following code to your HTML document (new code in bold).

```
<BODY>
    <DIV onclick = "readField()" id = "myText"> Hello World</DIV>
    First Name: <INPUT type = text id = "fName" onblur = "checkField()">
</BODY>
```

In the previous code:

- We just create a new text field and give it the ID **name**.

- We also associate the event **onblur** to this element which is triggered whenever the element goes out of focus; in other words, if the user clicks on (or types within) this element and then focuses on a different element by using the tab key or by clicking somewhere else in the document, the **onblur** event will occur.

- In this case, the function **checkField** will be called.

You can then add the following function within the **SCRIPT** tags.

```
function checkField()
{
    var fieldContent = document.getElementById("fName").value;
    if (fieldContent == "") alert ("Sorry, this field should not be empty");
}
```

In the previous code:

- We create a new function called **checkField**.

- Within this function, we access the value of the text field with the id **fName** and store it in the variable called **fieldContent**.

- In this case, we use the attribute of the node called **value**, which represents the content of the text field.

- We then check whether the content of the text field is empty; if this is the case, an alert message is displayed.

Adding Interaction

Once you have typed and saved your code, you can refresh the corresponding browser window; if you click on the empty text field and then click somewhere else on the page, an alert message should be displayed.

There are obviously many other DOM methods and they can be used to:

- Modify the CSS properties of a node.
- Modify the content of a node.
- Modify the attributes of a node (we will see that later).
- Create new nodes.
- Associate events to nodes.
- Modify the hierarchy of the document.

Let's look at some of these features, starting with modifying the CSS properties.

- Please, open the file **dom.html**.
- Modify the script as follows (new code in bold)

```
if (fieldContent == "")
{
        alert ("Sorry, this field should not be empty");
        document.getElementById("name").style.backgroundColor = "red";
}
```

In the previous code, we specify that, in addition to the alert message, the background of the text field should also be in red, if the user has left this field empty. For this purpose, we access the attribute called **style** for this node, which is associated to its *CSS* properties, and then access the **backgroundColor** attribute to set it to **red**.

Once you have typed and save your code, you can refresh the corresponding browser window; if you click on the empty text field and then click somewhere else on the page, an alert message should be displayed and the text field's background should also turn to red, as illustrated in the next figure.

Hello World
First Name: ▮▮▮▮▮▮▮▮▮▮

Figure 3-4: Modifying the background of a text field

There are, obviously, many other ways to select specific nodes (or elements) in your document, and this can be done using, for example, the following functions.

- **document.getElementsByTagName**: returns elements with the same tag name.

- **document.getElementsByClassName**: returns elements with the same class name.

- **document.querySelectorAll**: returns elements that correspond to a given CSS selector.

For more information about document functions and the DOM, you can look at the official documentation here: **https://developer.mozilla.org/en-US/docs/Web/API/Document** or **https://developer.mozilla.org/en-US/docs/Web/API/Document_Object_Model**.

Adding Interaction

USING JAVASCRIPT WITH FORMS (PART 2)

As we have seen previously, you can modify the attributes of any HTML element using JavaScript; this can be applied to the style of the elements, as we have seen in the previous section, but it can be expanded to other attributes also. For example, if your page includes an image, we could, through JavaScript, modify the attributes of the image including the attribute called **width** (i.e., the width of the image) or **src** (i.e., where the image is located).

Another interesting example of modifying attributes through JavaScript is when you work with forms. As you may have already come across forms, they are usually employed to gather data from the user and to then send it to a server. Forms usually include elements such as text fields, sliders, or radio buttons. For example, when you book a flight or a hotel room, you will more than likely use a form to provide your name, address and other useful information. In this case, you may notice that some fields will, for example, auto-complete; for example, if you select a specific country, the associated international code will automatically appear in the field that corresponds to the phone number. Or even better, you may be required to enter your billing address, and, to save you from re-entering the same information for the shipping address, you may avail of a button that, when clicked, copies your address details over to the shipping address. This is very useful as it improves the user experience, and it can be achieved through JavaScript.

So, in the next section, we will go through a very simple example of how such a form can be created and how JavaScript can be employed to customize it.

- Please create a new HTML document and save it as **booking.html**, or any other name of your choice.

- Add the following code to the body of the document.

```
<FORM>
      Billing Address<BR>
      <TABLE border = 0>
           <TR>
                <TD>First Name</TD><TD><INPUT id =  "s_fname"> </TD>
           </TR>
           <TR>
                <TD>Last Name</TD><TD><INPUT id =  "s_lname"> </TD>
           </TR>
           <TR>
                <TD>Shipping Address</TD><TD><INPUT id =  "s_address"> </TD>
           </TR>
      </TABLE>
      <BR><BUTTON type = "button"  onclick = "copyAddress();"> Same  Shipping  Details
</BUTTON><BR><BR>Billing Address<BR>
      <TABLE border = 0>
           <TR>
                <TD>First Name</TD><TD><INPUT id =  "b_fname"> </TD>
           </TR>
           <TR>
                <TD>Last Name</TD><TD><INPUT id =  "b_lname"> </TD>
           </TR>
           <TR>
                <TD>Shipping Address</TD><TD><INPUT id =  "b_address"> </TD>
           </TR>
           </TABLE>
</FORM>
```

In the previous code:

- We create a form that includes several fields for the shipping and billing address.

- The labels and text fields are formatted using a table (this is optional).

- A button labelled **"Same Shipping Details"** is provided so that the user can fill-in the billing details and decide to copy these over to the shipping details, if necessary.

- When this button is pressed, the function **copyAddress** is called and we will define this function later.

Note that all the text fields have an ID that will be employed later to copy the information from the billing section to the shipping section.

- Please add the following code to the head of the document:

Adding Interaction

```
<!DOCTYPE html>
<HTML >
    <HEAD>
        <SCRIPT>
            function copyAddress()
            {
                document.getElementById("b_fname").value = document.getElementById("s_fname").value;
                document.getElementById("b_lname").value = document.getElementById("s_lname").value;
                document.getElementById("b_address").value = document.getElementById("s_address").value;
            }
        </SCRIPT>
    </HEAD>
```

In the previous code:

- We declare the function **copyAddress**.

- When it has been called, it will copy the value (or the text) present in the field for the first name from the section **Billing Details** to the section **Shipping Details**.

- The same will be done for the fields **last name** and **address**.

Once you have completed the code, please save your file, and open it in a browser. After completing the fields **first name**, **last name** and **address** for the billing details, click on the button called "**Same Shipping Details**" and the shipping details should now be similar.

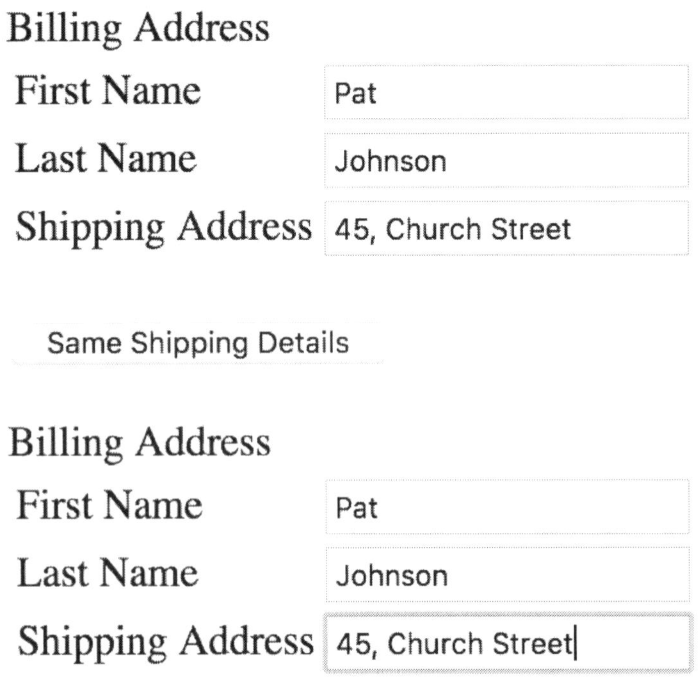

Billing Address

First Name | Pat
Last Name | Johnson
Shipping Address | 45, Church Street

Same Shipping Details

Billing Address

First Name | Pat
Last Name | Johnson
Shipping Address | 45, Church Street

Figure 3-5: using JavaScript to copy information

So at this stage, you probably see how JavaScript can really be useful when designing a page that improves the user experience.

88

VALIDATING FORMS WITH THE FORMS API

As we have seen in the previous sections, HTML provides forms that you can employ to collect information about the user. In addition, you can use JavaScript to access form fields, such as text fields, to read and copy information between fields, for example. This is very handy as it makes the user experience easier by preventing them from having to enter the same information twice.

In addition to improving the user experience, it is also very common to have to check the information entered by a user before it is sent to the server. This is often called **form validation** or the ability to ensure that all information entered in the different input fields of the form are as you (the developer) expect them to be. For example, you may want the user to enter only digits or letters in some fields, or you may expect the values entered to be within a specific range. For this purpose, JavaScript provides a built-in library of methods that can be used to check the validity of the content entered in the field and to display an error message in this case. Let's look at an example that illustrate these functionalities.

- Please create a new HTML page with a name of your choice, for example **validate_forms.html**.

- You may also check that it includes an HTML5 header, along with tags for the HEAD and the BODY of the document.

- Add the following code in the body of the document.

```html
<FORM>
      Phone Number: <INPUT type = "number" id = "phoneNumber" onblur = "checkField()"> <DIV id="feedback"></DIV>
</FORM>
```

In the previous code:

- We create a field for the user to enter a phone number.

- This field is of type **number**, which means that only numbers should be entered in this field.

- We provide an ID called **phoneNumber** to this field.

- We also specify that whenever the field is blurred, in other words when we leave this field, that the function **checkField** should be called.

- We also include a DIV with the ID **feedback** that is empty for now, but that will include feedback on the data entered by the user.

We can then define the function **checkField**, by adding the following code to the HEAD section of the document:

Adding Interaction

```
<SCRIPT>
function checkField()
{
    var fieldToValidate = document.getElementById("phoneNumber");
    var feedback = document.getElementById("feedback");
    if          (!fieldToValidate.checkValidity())          feedback.innerHTML     =
fieldToValidate.validationMessage;
}
</SCRIPT>
```

In the previous code:

- We declare a variable called **fieldToValidate** that will refer to the field with the ID called **phoneNumber**.

- We also create a variable called **feedback** that will be used for the feedback.

- We then check whether the data entered in the field for the phone number is valid using the method **checkValidity**.

- If the content of the field is not valid then we display a corresponding validation message in the feedback field.

- This feedback message is automatically provided by the browser.

This being said we could have modified this message to include our own message by replacing the last statement with the following:

```
if (!fieldToValidate.checkValidity()) feedback.innerHTML = "Looks like you have entered letters, please try again";
```

In the previous code, we set the feedback message to a string of our choice.

If you test this page, enter letters in the phone number field and then press the tab key, you should see that the border of the field for the phone number turns to red, and that a feedback message is displayed just below it, as illustrated in the next figures (depending on whether you are using the default error message or a custom message of your choice).

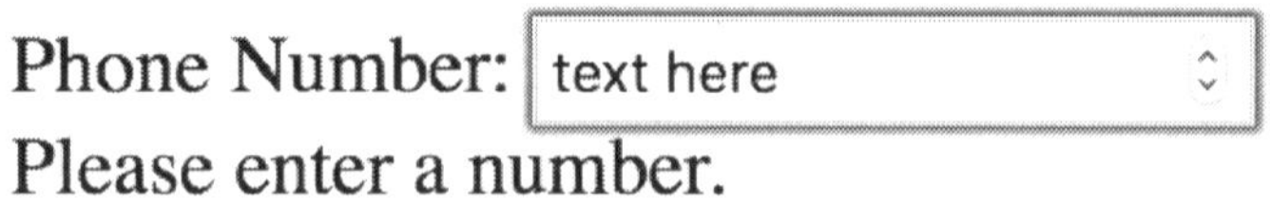

Phone Number: [text here]
Please enter a number.

Figure 3-6: Validating fields

Phone Number: [text here]
Looks like you have entered letters, please try again

Figure 3-7: Validating fields using custom feedback text

As you can see, this feature is very useful because it makes it possible to provide feedback to the user straight away.

While the previous example dealt with checking the general validity of a field, you can also perform other checks using the validity property of the field, such as:

- Checking if a required field is empty: the property is **valueMissing**.
- Checking if the information entered is too long: the property is **tooLong**.
- Check if the value is below the minimum value: the property is **rangeUnderflow**.
- Check if the value is beyond the maximum value: the property is **rangeOverflow**.

For example, if we wanted to make the phone number a required information (i.e., compulsory) and check whether the value was missing for the phone number, we could have modified our code as follows:

- Please modify the HTML code so that the field is mandatory (new code in bold).

```
Phone Number: <INPUT type = "number" id = "phoneNumber" onblur = "checkField()" required>
<DIV id="feedback"></DIV>
```

- Then modify the JavaScript code as follows:

```
if (fieldToValidate.validity.valueMissing) feedback.innerHTML = "This field can't be left empty. Please enter a value";
```

In the previous code, we access the **validity** property of the field, and the property called **valueMissing**. If **valueMissing** is true, then feedback is displayed in the corresponding field.

If you save this code and test the page by leaving the phone number field empty and by pressing the tab key, an error message should appear, as illustrated in the next figure.

Phone Number: [   ]
This field can't be left empty. Please enter a value

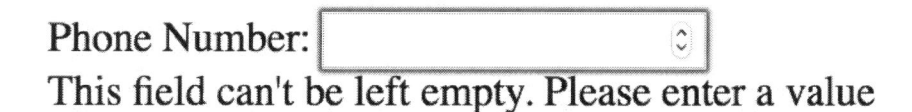

Figure 3-8: Checking required fields

For more information about form validation and custom error messages, please see the official page: https://developer.mozilla.org/en-US/docs/Learn/HTML/Forms/Form_validation.

Adding Interaction

EVENT LISTENERS

As we have seen in the previous sections, it is possible to define how an element will respond to a particular event. For example, we can specify the function that should be called when a button is clicked using the following code:

```
<Button type = "button" onclick = "doSomething()">Click Me </Button>
```

This is called inline events, because the even and its handler are specified in the HTML code on the same line.

However, there may be times when you may like to associate more than one event to an element (e.g., onclick, onblur, etc.) or specify how the event is processed when an element is nested within another element. In this case, using event listeners makes a lot of sense, so let's look at how we can use event listeners.

If we were to use event listeners for the button that we have created previously, we could do the following:

- Please create a new HTML document with the name **eventListener.html**, or any other name of your choice, using the usual structure (i.e., HEAD, BODY and SCRIPT sections) and modify the HTML code as follows:

```
<BODY onload = "initEvents()">
<BUTTON id = "button" type = "button" > Click me </BUTTON>
```

In the previous code:

- We specify that we can call the function **initEvents** when the document is loaded.

- As we will see later, the function **initEvents** will create event listeners for the button.

- We just create a button with an id; however, the statement **onclick** is not used here.

We can then define the functions that will deal with the events.

- Please add the two following functions within the <SCRIPT> tags:

```
function initEvents()
{
     document.getElementById("button").addEventListener ("click", displayMessage)
}
function displayMessage()
{
        console.log("You just selected the text field");
}
```

In the previous code:

- We create the function **initEvents** (called when the document is loaded).

92

Adding Interaction

- We specify that we will listen to the **click** event for the button with the id "**button**".

- When this event occurs, we will then call the function called **displayMessage**.

- In the function **displayMessage**, we then write a message in the console window.

> Note that the method **addEventListener** is not supported in Internet Explorer IE8 and earlier versions; in this case you can use the methods **attachEvent** (or **detachEvent** to remove/detach the event listener).

In a similar way, we could add another event listener to the button to detect if the mouse is over the button as follows by adding the following code to the function **initEvents**:

```
document.getElementById("button").addEventListener ("mouseover", displayMessageWhenOver);
```

In the previous code, we specify that whenever the mouse is over the button (i.e., the event **mouseover**), that we should call the function **displayMessageWhenOver**.

- We can then declare the function **displayMessageWhenOver** as follows.

```
function displayMessageWhenOver()
{
     console.log("You just moved the mouse over the button");
}
```

If you save your code, refresh the page and move the mouse over the button, a message should be displayed in the console window, saying "**You just moved the mouse over the button**".

So, as you can see, using event listeners, we can add multiple events to an element, with associated functions (or handlers). In addition, you may sometimes need to remove these events when you no longer want to detect these for a specific element; in this case, you can use the method called **removeEvent**, as follows:

- Please add the following line to the function **displayMessage**:

```
document.getElementById("button").removeEventListener ("mouseover", displayMessageWhenOver);
```

In the previous code, we just specify that we will no longer listen to the event **mouseover** for the button.

So after saving the code, you could do the following:

- Refresh the page.

- Move the mouse over the button; this should display the message "**You just moved over the button**" in the console window.

- Then click on the button; this will display the message "**You just clicked**".

- And then move the mouse over the button again; no additional messages should be displayed.

Adding Interaction

BUBBLING AND CAPTURING EVENTS

As illustrated previously, you can both add or remove events listeners to and from elements on your page. In addition, event listeners can also be used when elements are nested. When two or more elements are nested and include event listeners, it can be useful to specify which event will be processed first. In JavaScript terms, when we deal with the innermost element (i.e., the child), we say that we are bubbling events, and if we decide to deal with the outermost element (i.e., the parent), we say that we are capturing events.

By default, if you add an event to an element, events are bubbled; however, it is possible to modify this options when adding an event, by specifying a third attribute and setting it to true (for a **capturing** behavior).

Let' look at an example.

- Please add the following code to the HTML page.

```
<TABLE id = "table" style = "background-color: black">
        <TR><TD>Inside TR</TD><TD>Inside TR</TD><TD>Inside TR</TD></TR>
        <TR><TD>Inside TR</TD><TD id = "innerCell" style = "background-color: red">Click Me, I Am inside</TD><TD>Inside TR</TD></TR>
        <TR><TD>Inside TR</TD><TD>Inside TR</TD><TD>Inside TR</TD></TR>
</TABLE>
```

In the previous code:

- We create a table with a black background and with the ID **outterDiv**.

- We also create three rows, one of them includes a cell with the ID **innerDiv** and a red background.

- The idea is that the cell with the id **innerCell** (the child in this case) is inside the table, so that the table (the parent in this case) is higher in the hierarchy of the document.

Next, we can add the following code to the function **initEvents**.

```
document.getElementById("table").addEventListener ("click", displayMessageWhenTableClicked, false);
document.getElementById("innerCell").addEventListener ("click", displayMessageWhenInnerCellClicked, false);
```

In the previous code:

- We add event listeners to the table and to the cell with the ID **innerCell**.

- We are looking for the event called **click** (i.e., this is similar to the event **onclick** that we have used in the previous sections).

- We are using, as we have done before, the method **addEventListener**, but this time, we specify a third parameter that relates to whether the event should be captured or bubbled; so the event, here, will not be captured, but bubbled instead (i.e., the last parameter is set to false).

94

Adding Interaction

Next, we can add the following code within the SCRIPT tags:

```
function displayMessageWhenTableClicked()
{
          console.log("You clicked within the table");
}
function displayMessageWhenInnerCellClicked()
{
     console.log("You clicked within the cell");
}
```

If you save your code, and refresh the page in the browser window, it should look like the following figure.

Figure 3-9: Processing events

You can then and click on the inner cell (in red) you should see the following message in the console window.

```
You clicked within the cell
You clicked within the table
```

Figure 3-10: Bubbling events

This makes sense. The event from the cell is dealt with first, and then the event from the table is processed, as expected for a bubbling behavior.

Now, we could modify our code, to modify the way events are processed by modifying the **initEvents** function as follows (new code in bold).

```
document.getElementById("table").addEventListener ("click", displayMessageWhenTableClicked, true);
document.getElementById("innerCell").addEventListener ("click", displayMessageWhenInnerCellClicked, true);
```

In the previous code, the click events for the table and the inner cell will be captured rather than bubbled.

If you save your code, refresh the page and click on the inner cell (in red) you should see the following message in the console window.

95

Adding Interaction

```
You clicked within the table
You clicked within the cell
```

Figure 3-11: Capturing events

Again, this makes a lot of sense. The event from the table is dealt with first, and then the event from the inner cell is processed, as expected for a bubbling behavior.

Eh voila!

So as you can see, event listeners can be added to elements, and events are processed depending on how elements relate to each other or which one is the highest in the page hierarchy.

> If you are having troubles remembering the different modes (bubbling or capturing), think about bubbles rising from the bottom of the see to its surface. The root of your document is at the surface, and the more nodes you create within the document, and the further down you dive. As you are diving to the further-most elements, your bubbles will go up to the surface.

Adding Interaction

NAVIGATING THROUGH NODES

As you have seen in the previous sections, it is possible to access elements in your HTML document using what is often refereed as the DOM (Document Object Model) which is a hierarchy of the elements included in your page.

> A document includes a collection of nodes; nodes can be elements, whereby, an element is a node that is defined by tags and that have properties such as attributes or an id.

As we have seen previously, the content of an HTML page is seen as a collection of nodes or elements, that are organized in (and relate to each-other through) a hierarchy.

Depending on where they are in this hierarchy, each node can be a parent, a child, and/or a sibling. This relationship is defined based on the way elements are nested.

Let's take the following example:

```
<HTML>
    <HEAD>
    </HEAD>
    <BODY>
            <DIV id = "div1"> Hello World 1</DIV>
            <DIV id = "div2"> Hello World 2</DIV>
    </BODY>
<HTML>
```

In the previous code:

- All the elements in the document are nested within the <HTML> tag; therefore, the <HTML> node is called the root of the document as it doesn't have any parent.

- There are two elements directly nested under the <HTML> element, that is: <HEAD> and <BODY>; so <HEAD> and <BODY> are the children of <HTML>. Furthermore, as we read the document sequentially from top to bottom, <HEAD> is the first child (as it appears first) and <BODY> is the second child.

- The same applies to the element <BODY>: There are two DIVS nested directly under the <BODY> elements, that is the DIV with the ID **div1** and the div with the ID **div2**.

- Furthermore, the div with the ID div1 has text within **"Hello World 1"**; so **"Hello World 1"** is the child of the DIV with the ID **div1**.

- BODY and HEAD are siblings.

As you can see, an HTML document looks somehow like a family tree, with relations between the different nodes of the tree, and to be able to navigate through these, JavaScript provides a set of properties and methods that makes it possible to refer to a node and its parents, children, siblings, or its HTML content and to also modify the content of the document by adding, replacing, or removing specific nodes.

Adding Interaction

Some of the key attributes for nodes include the following:

- **parentNode**: returns the parent of a specific node.
- **childNodes**: returns the number of child nodes for a specific node.
- **firstChild**: returns a node that is the first child of the node.
- **lastChild**: returns a node that is the last child of the node.
- **nextSibbing**: returns a node that is the next sibling of the current node for a given parent.
- **previousSibbling**: returns a node that is the previous sibling of the current node for a given parent.

Let's look at those in the context of the code that we have just created.

- Please create a new HTML document with a name of your choice, for example **working_with_nodes.html**.
- Add the following code to the BODY of the document.

```
<BODY onload = countElements()>
        <DIV id = "div1"> Hello World 1</DIV><DIV id = "div2""> Hello World 2</DIV>
</BODY>
```

In the previous code, we specify that the function **countElements** should be called when the page is loaded. We also define two DIVs, each with a specific ID.

We can now define the function **countElements**:

- Please add the following code to the HEAD of your document.

```
function countElements()
    {
            var body = document.getElementsByTagName("BODY")[0];
            var parentOfBody = body.parentNode.nodeName;
            console.log("Parent of BODY is "+parentOfBody);
            var firstChild = body.firstChild.nodeName;
            console.log("First Child of BODY is"+firstChild);

            var lastChild = body.lastChild.nodeName;
            console.log("Last Child of BODY is "+lastChild);

            var nextSiblingOfId1 = document.getElementById("div1").nextSibling.nodeName;
            console.log("The next sibling of DIV1 is "+nextSiblingOfId1);
    }
```

In the previous code:

- We select the BODY element.
- We then look for the parent of this node and print its name.
- We also look for the first child of the BODY element and print its name.
- We the look for the last child of the BODY element and print its name.

Adding Interaction

- We then look for the next sibling of the element with the ID div1.

As you save your code and refresh the corresponding HTML page in your browser, you should see the following message.

```
Parent of BODY is HTML
First Child of BODY is#text
Last Child of BODY is DIV
The next sibling of DIV1 is DIV
```

Figure 3-12: Displaying relationships between nodes and elements

In the previous figure you can see that:

- The HTML node is seen as the parent of BODY, and that seems correct.

- The first child of BODY is seen as some text; and this is because we have included some text just after the <BODY> tag; this being said, for example sake, if we decided to remove the text after the BODY (between the body tag and the first div) tag as follows...

```
<BODY onload = countElements()><DIV id = "div1">
```

- ...the message in the console window would display that the DIV is the first child of the BODY element, that the last child of the body tag is seen as the last div and that the last sibling of the first DIV is a DIV, and that seems correct, based on our hierarchy.

Adding Interaction

ADDING AND REMOVING NODES AND ELEMENT

While in the previous sections we have looked at some of the properties of elements and nodes, these properties were read-only (i.e., we could not directly modify them).

This being said, you can also use specific methods to modify the document through the creation or modification of nodes, and some of these methods are as follows:

- **createElement**: creates a new element.

- **appendChild**: adds a child to a parent element; if the parent already has a child, then the new child will be inserted as the last element.

- **insertBefore**: inserts an element to a parent just before a specific child.

- **removeChild**: removes a child from the parent.

- **replaceChild**: replaces a child with another element.

Let's experiment with these.

- Please open the file that you have been using so far (e.g., **working_with_nodes.html**).

- Modify the BODY tag as follows:

```
<!-- <BODY onload = countElements()><DIV id = "div1"> Hello World 1</DIV><DIV id = "div2"">
Hello World 2</DIV> -->
         <BODY onload = modifyDocument()><DIV id = "div1"> Hello World 1</DIV><DIV id =
"div2""> Hello World 2</DIV>
```

In the previous code, we comment the previous instructions and we specify that the function **modifyDocument** should be called when the document is loaded.

We can now define the function **modifyDocument**:

- Please add the following code to the **SCRIPT** section within the **HEAD** of the document.

```
function modifyDocument()
{
     var newParagraph = document.createElement("P");
     var nodeWithinParagraphElement = document.createTextNode("This is a new paragraph");
     newParagraph.appendChild(nodeWithinParagraphElement);
     document.getElementById("div1").appendChild(newParagraph);
}
```

In the previous code:

- We declare the function **modifyDocument**.

- We create a new element called **newParagraph** that will be a paragraph. This is similar to creating a paragraph using the HTML tags <P> and </P>.

- We then create a text node (literally some text) and then add this text to the paragraph that we have created previously using the method **appendChild**.

- Finally, the paragraph (that now includes text) is added to the DIV with the ID 1

You can now save your code and refresh the corresponding page, and it will look like the following figure.

Hello World 1

This is a new paragraph

Hello World 2

Figure 3-13: Adding nodes through JavaScript

As we have seen before, the method **appendChild** adds a child to a parent element; if this parent already has a child, then the new one will be inserted as the last element. So we could try to use the method **inserBefore** instead to see how it works.

- Please add the following code at the end of the function **modifyDocument**.

```
var newParagraph2 = document.createElement("P");
var nodeWithinParagraphElement2 = document.createTextNode("This is a new paragraph that will appear before the previous one");
newParagraph2.appendChild(nodeWithinParagraphElement2);
document.getElementById("div1").insertBefore(nodeWithinParagraphElement2, newParagraph);
```

The previous code is similar to the code we have previously created; the key difference lies in the last line whereby we specify that the node called **nodeWithParagraphElement2** will be added to the DIV parent, but this insertion will be performed just before the node called **newParagraph**.

You can save your code and refresh the corresponding browser page, and the it should look like the next figure.

Hello World 1This is a new paragraph that will appear before the previous one

This is a new paragraph

Hello World 2

Figure 3-14: Adding nodes using insertBefore

Adding Interaction

Last but not least, we could also experiment with removing nodes from the document using the method **removeChild**.

- Please add the following code to the BODY of the document.

```
<BUTTON onclick = "removeNodes()" type = button> Click here to remove paragraphs.</BUTTON>
```

- Add the following function to the SCRIPT tag that is in the HEAD of the document.

```
function removeNodes()
{
        var firstDiv = document.getElementById("div1");
        if (firstDiv.firstChild) firstDiv.removeChild(firstDiv.firstChild);
}
```

In the previous code:

- We define the function **removeNodes**.

- We then create a new variable called **firstDiv** that will refer to the element with the ID **div1**.

- We then check whether this element has children.

- If this is the case, we then remove the first children of this element.

- You can now save your script, refresh the page and press the button; you should see that the text from the DIV with the ID **div1** will disappear progressively, starting with the text "**Hello World 1**", followed by "**This is a new paragraph that will appear before the previous one**", then followed by the text "**This is a new paragraph**".

WORKING WITH THE BROWSER

As we have seen in the last sections, JavaScript provides some very interesting tools to deal with the user's actions, and to also modify an HTML document. In addition, JavaScript also makes it is possible to access information from the user's browser. This information can be related to:

- The browser's information: its version and the user's operating system, for example.

- The window: to be able to open, close or resize a window.

- The screen: to access the screen's width, height, color and pixel depth.

- The location: to access information related to the document's current location and to be able to load a new page or access a page previously open.

- The history: to access previous pages already open by the user.

- Messages such as prompts or alerts.

In the next sections, we will look at some of these functionalities in detail.

Adding Interaction

DISPLAYING INFORMATION ABOUT THE BROWSER

So first, let's look at the browser information. From JavaScript, it is possible to gather different types of information about the browser, including the operating system, whether Java is enabled or whether the browser is online. This can be done through the object **window.navigator**.

Let's look at the following example:

- Please create a new HTML document and add the following code in the HEAD of the document; you could, for example save this page as **browserInfo.html**.

```
<SCRIPT>
displayBrowserInfo();
function displayBrowserInfo()
{
    var message = "Online status: "+navigator.onLine;
    message += "\nJava Enabled: "+navigator.javaEnabled();
    message+="\nYour Operating System: "+navigator.platform;
    alert (message);
}
</SCRIPT>
```

In the previous code:

- We declare a function called **displayBrowserInfo**.

- In this function, we create a message that includes information about the browser.

- This information includes the online status, whether Java is enabled, and the operating system.

- We then call this function.

- Note that we use **\n** in some of the strings so that new text is written on a new line for clarity.

> Note that you can use **window.navigator** or **navigator** interchangeably.

You can save your page, and refresh the corresponding web page, and a message similar to the following should be displayed.

```
Online status: true
Java Enabled: false
Your Operating System: MacIntel
```

[OK]

Figure 3-15: Displaying information about the browser

There are many more methods and attributes available for the object **window.navigator**, and you can see them on the official documentation here: **https://developer.mozilla.org/en-US/docs/Web/API/Navigator**.

Adding Interaction

OPENING, CLOSING AND MOVING WINDOWS FROM A SCRIPT

In addition to gathering information about the browser, JavaScript also makes it possible, amongst other things, to open, close, resize or move windows, through the **window** object. Opening and closing windows can be very useful in your pages, when you'd like to display contextual messages, for example.

In the following example, we will create a window and move it thanks to the buttons that we will create.

- Please add the following code to the BODY of the document that you have created in the previous section.

```
<BUTTON onclick = "openWindow()" type = "button">Click to open a new window</BUTTON>
<BUTTON onclick = "closeWindow()" type = "button">Click to close the new window</BUTTON>
```

In the previous code, we create two buttons and each of them will be used to open or close a window that has already been created.

- Please add the following code to the HEAD of the document:

```
function openWindow()
{
     myWindow = window.open("","hello", "menubar=yes,location=yes,resizable=yes,scrollbars=yes,status=yes, width=300, height = 300");
}
function closeWindow()
{
     myWindow.close();
}
```

In the previous code:

- We create two functions **openWindow** and **closeWindow**.

- The first function called **openWindow** creates a global variable called **myWindow**; it is created as a global variable because there is no **var** keyword beforehand, and it will refer to a window created using the method **window.open**.

As you can see, the method **window.open** takes several parameters, separated by a comma:

- The first parameter is the **url** of the page to be displayed in our new window; in our case, there is no url associated so the parameter is left blank (i.e., this will be a blank page).

- The second parameter is the name of the new window; in our case, this will be **"hello"**.

- The third parameter is a string within which you can specify more information about the new window; each of these consist of a pair composed of a parameter and its corresponding value; in our case, we specify that the window will include a menu bar, that the location will be displayed, that the window will be resizable, with a status bar, with a width of 300pixels and a height of 300pixels.

- The function **closeWindow** closes the window that we have just created.

Adding Interaction

> Note that not all parameters need to be specified when you create the window and you can decide which parameter you would like to set. To find a list of all possible options/parameters when creating a new window, please see the official documentation for all the features available here: **https://developer.mozilla.org/en-US/docs/Web/API/Window/open**

Now that we know how to open and close a window, we could try to move it; here is how:

- Please add the following code to the BODY of the document.

```
<BUTTON onclick = "moveWindowRight()" type = "button">Click to move new window to the right</BUTTON>
<BUTTON onclick = "moveWindowLeft()" type = "button">Click to move new window to the left</BUTTON>
```

In the previous code, we create two buttons that will be used to move the new window to the left or to the right.

We can now create the two methods **moveWindowLeft** and **moveWindowRight** by adding the following code to the HEAD of the document, within the SCRIPT section:

```
function moveWindowRight()
{
    myWindow.moveBy(100,0);
    myWindow.focus();
}
function moveWindowLeft()
{
    myWindow.moveBy(-100,0);
    myWindow.focus();
}
```

In the previous code:

- We declare two functions **moveWindowLeft** and **moveWindowRight**.

- Both functions use the method **moveBy**.

- In the function **moveWindowRight** we move the window **myWindow** to the right by specifying the amount of pixels on the x- (100 pixels) and y-axes (0 pixels).

- The same applies to the function **moveWindowLeft**.

- We also ensure that the new window is visible by calling the method **focus**.

You can now save your code and refresh the corresponding browser window; you should see that the page now includes four buttons. You can then create a new window (by pressing the corresponding button), the new window should be at the forefront; then move the window to the right by pressing the corresponding button several times.

Adding Interaction

> Note that you can also use the method **window.moveTo** to move the window to a specific position onscreen.

A new window can also be resized either in relation to its original size or by providing an absolute new width and height. Let's look at both of these techniques.

- Please add the following code to the BODY of your document.

```
<BUTTON onclick = "resizeWindow()" type = "button">Click to Resize the new window</BUTTON>
```

- Please add the following code to the HEAD of the document, with the SCRIPT section.

```
function resizeWindow()
{
    mywindow.resizeTo(500, 500);
    mywindow.focus();
}
```

In the previous code:

- We declare the function **resizeWindow**.

- In this function we resize the new window so that its width and height are both 500 pixels.

- We then give the focus to this window so that it is visible.

Please save your code, refresh the corresponding browser window, and you should see that the page now includes five buttons; you can then create a new window (by pressing the corresponding button), the new window should be at the forefront; then resize the window by pressing the corresponding button. You should then see that the size of the window has increased.

We could also resize the window relative to its original size by just modifying your code as follows (new code in bold):

```
function resizeWindow()
{
    //mywindow.resizeTo(500, 500);
    mywindow.resizeBy(-400, -400);
    mywindow.focus();
}
```

In the previous code, we just use the method **resizeBy**, and specify that the window's width and height should be 400 pixels shorter.

The methods that we just studied should give you a good start. This being said, there are obviously many more methods that can be used to work with windows in JavaScript, and you can see more information on the **window** object on the official documentation here:

https://developer.mozilla.org/en-US/docs/Web/API/Window

WORKING WITH THE BROWSER'S LOCATION AND HISTORY

In the previous sections we have managed to create a new window and to also move or resize this window from JavaScript. In this section, we will look at some other interesting features offered by JavaScript in terms of changing the current page from your code based on a new url or using the browser's history.

First let's look at how you can simply load a new page within the current window.

- Please create a new HTML document, with the usual structure (i.e., HEAD, BODY, and SCRIPT sections) and rename it **location_history.html** (or any other name of your choice).

- Add the following code to the BODY of the document.

```
<BODY >
    <BUTTON onclick = "changeLocation()" type = "button">Click to open go to Apple.com</BUTTON>
</BODY>
```

In the previous code we create a button that will call the function **changeLocation** when pressed.

- Please add the following code to the HEAD of the document

```
<SCRIPT>
    function changeLocation()
    {
            window.location.assign("http://www.apple.com");
    }
</SCRIPT>
```

In the previous code, we define the function **changeLocation** that opens a new url (i.e., a web address) in the current window.

After saving your page and opening it in a browser window, you can click on the button present on the page and you should see that the page **apple.com** is loaded.

An interesting way to implement this feature is for site redirection, when you'd like the visitor to be redirected to a website of your choice after a few seconds.

To experiment with this feature, please add the following code just before the function **changeLocation**.

```
setInterval(changeLocation, 1000);
```

In the previous code, we just specify that the function **changeLocation** should be called after 1 second (i.e., 1000 milliseconds).

After saving your code and refreshing the corresponding page, you should see that the site **apple.com** opens after 1 second.

As you can see, it is very easy to change the current location of your page from your script. In addition, it is also possible to set a new location that is based on your history (i.e., previous pages visited). Let's look at the following example:

Adding Interaction

- Please comment the following code in the HEAD of the document.

```
//setInterval(changeLocation, 1000);
```

- Add the following code to the HEAD of the document, within the SCRIPT section.

```
function goBack()
{
        window.history.back();
}
function goForward()
{
        window.history.forward();
}
```

In the previous code, we create two functions called **goBack** and **goForward**; the former, when called will navigate forward in your history, whereas the latter will navigate back.

- Please add the following code to the body of the document.

```
<BUTTON onclick = "goBack()" type = "button">Go Back</BUTTON>
<BUTTON onclick = "goBack()" type = "button">Go Forward</BUTTON>
```

- Save you code.

- Duplicate this HTML page and call the duplicate **location_history2.html**, for example.

- Make sure that these two files are saved in the same directory.

Finally, edit the first file (i.e., **location_history.html**) to add the following code to the BODY of the document.

```
<A href = "./location_history2.html"> Link to second page</A>
```

In the previous code, we create a hypertext link, whereby the user is redirected to the page location_history2.html after pressing the text "**link to second page**".

Once this is done, please open the first page (i.e., **location_history.html**) in a browser, and click on the link "**Link to second page**", this should open the second page; you can now press the button labelled "**back**" and it should take you back to the first page.

LEVEL ROUNDUP

SUMMARY

In this chapter, we have managed to add more interactivity to your web pages by adding and processing events. We looked into how to process events such as clicks or mouse movements. Building on this knowledge, you created simple programs where the browser processes actions from the user, and you created some code that made it possible to add information and content to the document from JavaScript. So we have covered some significant ground here: well done!

Quiz

It is now time to test your knowledge. Please specify whether the following statements are TRUE or FALSE. The answers are available on the next page.

1. The method **getElementByID** returns an element based on its ID.//
2. The event **onload** is called when the page has been loaded.
3. JavaScript provides default functions check the validity of a field within a form.
4. An element can only be associated to one event.
5. In terms of event-handling, when we deal with the innermost elements first, we say that we are bubbling events.
6. In terms of event-handling, when we deal with the outermost elements first, we say that we are capturing events.
7. DOM stands for Document Organization Model.
8. By default, if a parent has children and a new child is added using **appendChild**, this new child will become the last children.
9. Nodes can be removed using the method **removeChildren**.
10. An element is a node that is defined by tags and that have properties such as attributes or an id.

Solutions to the Quiz

1. TRUE.
2. TRUE.
3. TRUE.
4. FALSE.
5. TRUE.
6. TRUE.
7. FALSE.
8. TRUE.
9. FALSE (it's **removeChild**).
10. TRUE.

Adding Interaction

Checklist

You can move to the next chapter if you can do the following:

- Create new nodes from JavaScript.
- Create an event listener.
- Create a new window from JavaScript.

Challenge 1

Now that you have managed to complete this chapter and that you have gathered interesting skills, let's put these to the test. This particular challenge will get you to become more comfortable with adding elements from JavaScript. The solutions are included in the resource pack.

- Create a function that adds a new label and text field (an element of type INPUT) when it is called.
- These new elements will be created within an existing DIV
- After being created, this new element's type will be set to text (i.e., a text field).
- Call this function when a button from the page has been clicked.
- The label will include the text **"Field"** followed by a number; for example: Field 1, Field 2, and so on. So you will need to create a counter that is a global variable

Challenge 2

- Create a button that deletes the last text field and its corresponding label.
- Call this function when a second button labelled **"Delete Field"** has been pressed.
- If a new field is created by pressing the first button, the numbering should restart at the correct number.

4
THANK YOU

I would like to thank you for completing this book. I trust that you are now comfortable with coding in JavaScript. This book is of course only a Beginner's guide to get started with JavaScript; if you'd like to know more about JavaScript, you may try some of my other books available from the official page: **http://learnjavascriptforbeginners.wordpress.com**.

So that the book can be constantly improved, I would really appreciate your feedback and hear what you have to say. So, please leave me a helpful review on Amazon letting me know what you thought of the book and also send me an email (learnjavascriptforbeginners@gmail.com) with any suggestion you may have. I read and reply to every email.

Thanks so much!!

Printed in Great Britain
by Amazon